WISDOM
of the
ANCIENT SAGES

Mundaka Upanishad

WISDOM
of the
ANCIENT SAGES

Mundaka Upanishad

SWAMI RAMA

HIMALAYAN
INSTITUTE®

HONESDALE, PENNSYLVANIA USA

Himalayan Institute
952 Bethany Turnpike
Honesdale, PA 18431

HimalayanInstitute.org

Printed in the United States of America

23 22 21 20 19 18   4 5 6 7 8

ISBN-13: 978-0-89389-120-6 (paper)

Library of Congress Cataloging-in-Publication Data: CIP 90-48615

Rama, Swami, 1925-1996
      The wisdom of the ancient sages: Mundaka Upanishad / Swami
      Rama
            p. Cm.
            Includes translation of: Mundakopanisad.
            Includes index.
            1. Upanishads. Mundakopanisad—Commentaries.
      I. Upanishads.
            Mundakopanisad. English. 1990. II. Title.
            BL1124.7.M866R35 1990
            294.5'9218—dc20

This paper meets the requirements of ANSI/NISO Z39-48-1992
(Permanence of Paper).

Contents

The Profound Teachings of the Ancient Sages:
Mundaka Upanishad

The Vedic literature is perhaps the most ancient record in the library of man today. This literature is like a tropical forest, full of dense vegetation. Only a fortunate few persisted in their journey on this terse, tough, and abstruse path. After going through the dense forest, the seeker comes to the garden of Eden. Here, the sages enjoyed the eternal fragrance of the immortal flowers found in the garden on their way to the final goal of enlightenment. It is true that when an aspirant makes sincere effort and follows the disciplines of the spiritual path with mind, action, and speech, he or she is rewarded by the discovery of those eternal blossoms.

After the study of the vast, profound Vedic literature, these aspirants discovered the knowledge of the Upanishads. The subject matter of these great scriptures is beyond sense perception, and even the mind cannot fully grasp it. These teachings are not at all dogmatic; they are universal and transcend the limitations of time, space, and causation.

The knowledge of the Upanishads is perennial, though it

2 Wisdom of the Ancient Sages

varies in the nature of its symbols, imagery, and illustrations. Those aspiring to study these scriptures must first learn to interpret these symbols, images, and illustrations correctly and exactly.

The teachings of the Upanishads have a central theme—*moksha*—final emancipation or liberation. These teachings are as ever-young, ever-fresh, and evergreen as they were thousands of years ago. The entire Upanishadic literature leads the aspirant to understand and to be aware of the identity of *atman* with *Brahman*— the individual spirit with Absolute Truth. It is a fundamental and central theme.

There are *mahavakyas,* great and profound sayings, in the Upanishads, such as *"Tat tvam asi*—Thou art That." *"Aham brahmasmi*—I am Brahman." *"Sarvam khalu idam brahman*— All this is Brahman." However, if one is not prepared for these teachings, he or she will not be able to understand the apparent contradictions. Actually, they are not contradictions, but stages of *sadhana* (spiritual practice).

This literature is meant for all mankind, for those who are tirelessly making an effort to peek into the corridor of the future. They can prepare themselves to follow the discipline according to the Upanishadic literature. Many modern aspirants find themselves lost in the apparent reality and are dissatisfied with the musty fumes emanating from the world's atmosphere these days. People all over the world yearn to take a fresh breath, and to do so, they must dive into the depths of Upanishadic literature. Surely, they will find pearls of wisdom there and come into contact with the immortal breath, which is the very source of the universe.

Worn and tired, a seeker tries to find the solution for the great riddles of life that present themselves. He or she will certainly find an answer in the depths of the Upanishadic literature.

The Upanishads say, "look within, find within, and see within." It is in our innermost recess, in the innermost chamber of our being, that we find calmness, happiness, bliss, and wisdom. When a seeker realizes that his innermost atman is Brahman, then all his fetters are destroyed and he attains absolute freedom.

The Upanishadic teachings are like flowers gathered from the garden of the limitless. The seers, the competent teachers of the Upanishads, merely strung a thread through these flowers, so that every teaching became a garland. Today's world is passing through a serious crisis: stress, unhappiness, and disease are increasing. Mankind has forgotten the ancient landmark of its noble history. The present is restless, the future is vague, and it seems that we are all heading toward a dark age.

This leads us to believe that the present struggle will give birth to a new hope, which will help the flower of humanity to bloom and to attain its next step of civilization. We seem to be in a whirlpool of stagnant water. Thinkers who are concerned with the suffering of mankind feel that the present confusion and struggle may lead us to a positive phase, in which we see the dawn of a new light, which will guide and shape the future of mankind toward its final destination.

Modern scientists have been looking for new methods to spiritualize the conclusions of the physical sciences. Perhaps the wisdom and philosophy of the Upanishads will fulfill this need and show light to those who are aware of the darkness prevailing all around. We human beings have created much confusion by joining the crowded procession of life, which seems to have become utterly unmanageable.

I hope that modern men and women come home soon and understand the value of the ancient discoveries. They need to become aware of the fact that life has two aspects—within and without. Then, the physical sciences can become the means to comfort the human being, while the ancient sciences, like the wise teachings of the Upanishads, will help him to unfold his innermost potential and enable him to fathom the deeper aspects of his being. Without constructing this bridge of understanding—between within and without, between ancient and modern—real happiness, peace, and bliss are unattainable.

THE UPANISHADS

As we noted earlier, the Vedas are the most ancient scriptures in the possession of mankind today. They are also considered to be literary monuments. The word *veda* comes from its Sanskrit root, *vid,* which means "to know" or "wisdom." It is the fountainhead of superconscious wisdom. These scriptures preserve the utterances of the wisdom which is known as *Shabda Brahman,* revelation.

The *Brahmins* were the custodians of these scriptures, which are eternal and are considered to be without human authorship: "The Lord of life and of the universe brings forth the universe with the help of the knowledge of the Vedas." It is the Lord, the Manifester, who spontaneously brings forward knowledge, like the spontaneous and effortless breathing of the human being.

The *Mundaka Upanishad* explains that in the beginning of the universe, the Lord taught the knowledge of the Vedas to *Brahma,* the first born. When Brahma was in deep meditation, there arose a sound, AUM, which is considered to be the essence of Vedic wisdom. This sacred syllable transformed itself into the various sounds—the vowels and consonants of the alphabet. Brahma, assisted by the alphabet, uttered the words known as the Vedic hymns and mantras. Thus, the ancients came to possess the revelations of the Vedas.

The Vedic utterances are called *shrutis*, which means "to hear," since they were heard in deep meditation by the great seers and sages and the same knowledge was transmitted by preceptors to their disciples. For many centuries, these teachings were orally handed down, transmitted only by preceptor to disciple.

The Vedic wisdom has two major divisions—*karma kanda* and *jnana kanda*. The first deals with *karma*, ritualistic action, and matters such as sacrifice. These provide a means and lead one to material prosperity on earth and felicity in heaven after death. The knowledge of the external world and the actions performed therein help one to know life here and hereafter. The latter— jnana kanda—explains the methods of knowing the higher dimensions of life, through which one attains final liberation and the highest good.

Simultaneously, the institution of truth and learning, which was called *Vyasa*, grew. Brahma commanded the learned masters of that tradition, who were known as Vyasa, to compile this huge body of Vedic literature. Vyasa is also considered to be the author of the *Mahabharata*, of which the *Bhagavad Gita* is a unique slice that is well-known for its profound philosophy on the art of living and being.

Vyasa compiled the Vedas in a systematic and organized manner and arranged the sacred teachings into four books— the *Rig, Yajur, Sama,* and *Atharva Vedas.* Thus, Vyasa is simply a compiler of the Vedas and not the author.

The Vedic knowledge was revealed to the great seers and sages of the remote past, whose minds and hearts were purified by spiritual disciplines and who had fully concentrated minds and perfect control over themselves. Such great seers were called *rishis*— "seers of truth." There were both men and women among the rishis. It is worthy to note that during the Vedic period there was no distinction or discrimination between men and women in that both equally shared in spiritual life and attained spiritual heights.

The Vedas fall into two sections—Mantra and Brahmana. The Mantra section is also called Samhita, which means "putting together," or a collection. It is a compilation of hymns and prayers used in sacrificial ceremonies, the most important of which was the *soma* sacrifice. This was a highly sophisticated ceremony performed by the ancients to commune with and come in contact with the finer forces of nature, which are sometimes called gods or higher powers. The word *sacrifice* refers to the process of sacrificing the fruits of one's actions.

The Brahmana literature contains rules and regulations concerning the precise methods of performing ceremonies. The further development of the Brahmana literature was the Aranyaka, also termed "forest treatise," which gave guidelines to the forest dwellers. The forest dwellers did not have the resources to obtain the physical objects for rituals. Their way of worship was symbolic and internal and so were their methods of meditation. Their methods of worship were lifted to the mental level and then, finally, to the spiritual level.

According to the Vedic period, the normal lifespan of a human being was considered to be at least a hundred years, and it was divided into four stages—*brahmacharya,* the life of a student, was the first twenty-five years; *grahasthya,* the life of a householder, was another twenty-five years; *vanaprasthya,* the life of the forest dweller, twenty-five years, and the last twenty-five years were reserved for *sannyasa,* or renunciation.

During the first twenty-five years, a student was taught the importance of celibacy and then remained celibate by being austere and chaste. He or she then learned the art of living and being in the world, but also became aware of the goal of life—ultimate Truth. He served his teacher with humility. After completing his studies, he was commanded by his teacher not to deviate from truthful actions and to perform his duties righteously, being conscious of Brahman all the time.

Being a householder was merely a preparatory stage on the path of action, and not the whole life. During this period, the wife and husband participated in the sacrificial ritual, worshipping and living like the twin laws of life. The couple was like a beautiful chariot, of which the wife and husband were two wheels. There was a perfect understanding between them, and the institution of marriage was not only the means for pleasures and joys, but also the means for liberation. It was not intended for the partners to develop attachment or create bondage for themselves or each other.

The third stage, vanaprasthya, commenced when the hair turned gray and the face began to wrinkle. The couple assigned their responsibilities to their grown children and then retired to the forest dwellings.

The final stage, sannyasa, was the culmination of the restricted way of life, in which one renounced all the worldly cares and desires that create obstacles on the path of self-realization. When one becomes a wandering monk, attaining freedom from all attachments and desires, he absorbs himself in uninterrupted contemplation and directly experiences the non-duality of Brahman—Absolute Truth. In such a state of realization, the individual spirit becomes one with the cosmic spirit.

Such monks or renunciates dedicate their lives to truth with mind, action, and speech, and thus guide and serve humanity. These sannyasins are the spiritual leaders and guides of the masses of India today. It is actually for these great renunciates that the Upanishads—the concluding portion of the Aran-yakas—were intended.

The Upanishadic teachings expound on the direct experi-ence of Absolute Truth—Brahman—which liberates the aspi-rant from the bondage of karma, attachment, pain, and misery, and finally from all ignorance. The exalted wisdom of the Upa-nishads becomes the guidelines for a renunciate.

The Upanishads are also called the "Vedanta," the cream of the Vedas, because in them the Vedic wisdom attains its final culmination. It is difficult to say exactly when and how Vedic literature came into existence. According to the traditional view, the knowledge contained in all four Vedas is revealed and has existed from the very beginning of the creation cycle. Thus, the Vedas are not regarded as a philosophical development or an evolution in the process of thought.

The Vedas were later fragmented into many recensions because their revised, condensed teachings were imparted by various teachers. These recensions may differ from one another in content, but the central theme remains unchanged—that of self-realization.

It is also difficult to say when the Vedas were formally compiled. Some Western Indologists have assigned the Vedas to 2000 B.C. Max Muller estimated their compilation at about 1200 B.C., and another scholar, Haug, in 2400 B.C. Tilak, an eminent Indian scholar who used calculations based on astro-nomical data, says that the Vedic mantras were compiled five thousand years before the Christian era. Thus, the date of the Vedic hymns and collections remains essentially unknown, with the *Rig Veda* being the most ancient of all.

For thousands of years, these sacred books were not commit-ted to writing, and because of this, there has been a lamentable loss of material. It is difficult to say how many Upanishads are fully authentic. The authentication of an Upanishad is a complex process; their authenticity is supported by shrutis, which are regarded as and agreed to be authentic.

The word *Upanishad* has been misused by many religious leaders and scholars who have called their writings "Upanishad" in order to claim spiritual authority. Egotistical modern religious leaders, too, often call their writings "Upanishad." At the time of Akbar, the emperor of India in the sixteenth century, scholars had composed an Upanishad called *Allah Upanishad.* The *Muktika Upanishad,* which has its source in the *Yajur Veda,* declares that there are 108 Upanishads. Still other researchers and scholars claim that there are 208 Upanishads. But Shankara, the great scholar and architect of *Advaita* (non-dual) philosophy, commented only on ten principal Upanishads.

The wisdom of the Upanishads, the *Brahma Sutras,* and the *Bhagavad Gita* constitute the teachings of Vedanta. There are three main schools of Vedanta that still exist today: the dualist, the qualified non-dualist, and the non-dualist. Their expounders—Madhava, Ramanuja, and Shankara—all wrote commentaries on the principal Upanishads.

Shankara lived from 788-820 A.D. He won wide acceptance and prestige among all the scholars of India, and due to his rational approach, Advaita philosophy became popular among the scholars of India and later, the West. His commentaries on the Upanishads express a philosophy that is a great contribution to the wisdom of the world.

By the time the sun of Buddhism had already passed below the horizon, the aliens who had come to India had adopted Buddhism and begun to distort it. Shankara established a synthesis between Brahmanism and Buddhism, and at this critical juncture, he began to propagate the ideals of Advaita. He began his teaching while only five years of age and was considered to be a divine *avatara,* possessing a keen intellect and being endowed with immense spiritual power and knowledge. A wandering monk, he travelled far and wide to all the corners of India. He challenged the scholars of his time and cut through the cobwebs of narrow thinking by giving a rational and logical interpretation of the sacred texts.

Within the short time span of thirty-two years, he reformed the ancient order of renunciates and wrote commentaries on the Upanishads, the *Brahma Sutras,* and the *Bhagavad Gita.* He composed many hymns that are still sung by the scholars and aspirants of India today. These hymns inspire the heart and purify the spirit of the aspirant. His catholicity of heart and austere purity of intellect are unparalleled.

What is true in one place may be untrue in another place, at another time; that which is lawful in one time may be unlawful in another time. The teachings that bind a society into a whole and sustain it in one age may choke it in another age. Social, religious, and economic conditions change, as do society's laws and social rules of conduct. Over a span of time, these structures need modification and recasting, and yet a fresh interpretation, if not given precisely and correctly, may become injurious to the whole society and ultimately strangle the social organism. We can find an example of this in nature: if the bark of a tree is not protected, the tree's growth is stunted. At the same time, it is important for the growth of the living tree to shed the old bark and make a new living layer of bark for itself.

All societies of the world are suffering in some ways today. There are a number of reasons for this. First, the priests, preachers, and leaders of various orders do not have clarity of mind or purity of heart. Second, they interpret the great religious scriptures for their own benefit. Third, these leaders become fanatics because they do not study the scriptures of other religious groups. They are afraid to study other scriptures because they lack open minds. They are afraid of losing their following, and they don't propagate the universality of their religion. Fundamentally, all religions are one and the same and have their origin in only one Absolute Truth, without a second. Religions differ only in nonessentials. Finally, the "priestly wisdom" leads to false doctrines, which misguide the innocent masses. Thus, the truth contained in the scriptures remains obscure.

It is also important to note that the seeming irrelevance of the religious traditions of the world today proceeds from their inability to separate essentials from nonessentials—to distinguish the dead rules of the past from the spiritual truths of all times.

No religion of the world can regain its past glory, prestige, and dignity until it is prepared to face modification in the same spirit as modern science does. Its principles may be eternal, but its expressions certainly require modifications.

The ancient sages of the Vedic lore developed a *dharma,* or path of right living, which is called *sanatana dharma,* the eternal religion, because it derives its authority from its truth and eternal and impersonal character, rather than from any particular person.

From time to time, there come great avataras and leaders who we call incarnations. According to history and Vedic literature, these incarnations actually hold a second place to the seers. The seers of the Vedic period, who are *mantra drastha* (those who directly experienced truth), are considered to be higher than any incarnation.

It is important to note that Lord Krishna, the codifier of the *Bhagavad Gita,* borrowed and modified most of his teachings from the Upanishads. The seers and sages of the Vedic period were recorders of the truth. The Vedic shrutis are impersonal. That is why the ancients called their religion eternal, because the Vedas themselves are eternal.

The Meaning of Upanishad

The word *Upanishad* is derived from its root, *shad,* to which are added two prefixes, *upa* and *ni.* The prefix *upa* denotes nearness and *ni,* totality. The word *shad* is interpreted in three ways: 1) to loosen (the bondage of attachment), 2) to attain (final emancipation), and 3) to annihilate (the *samskaras* and ignorance—or *avidya*—exactly as light annihilates darkness).

The etymological meaning of the word *shad* is "knowledge" or *vidya,* which is received through a competent teacher. It completely loosens the bondage of the world and the ties of attachment and thus enables aspirants to realize the true Self. This knowledge completely destroys the ignorance that dismays and deludes the self-awareness of the Infinite, so that it comes to see itself as a finite, embodied creature.

The root *shad* with the prefix *upa* also connotes the humility with which the pupil should approach the preceptor. The Upanishadic knowledge is considered to be the sovereign science. It is a profound secret—the secret of secrets. The aspirant should know that the instructions given in the Upanishads are condensed formulas and they are *satyasya satyam*—the Truth of truths.

The Upanishads use the phrase "*neti, neti*—not this, not this," which means that an aspirant should not stop making sincere effort or be satisfied with the knowledge he has already received from various levels or internal states. There are various subtle levels of knowledge, but the final is the knowledge of Absolute Truth.

In ancient times, the preceptors of the Vedic lore were very cautious in imparting the secret vidyas, such as *prana vidya,* which is mentioned in the *Kathopanishad* or *madhu vidya* in *Brihadaranyaka Upanishad.* They would impart this knowledge only to those fortunate few who were fully prepared to receive this knowledge—those who had already done the preliminary spiritual practices, which are the very foundation of spirituality.

This vidya was not imparted to merely anyone, even if a person were willing to give the whole sea-girt earth full of treasures, for the treasure of Upanishadic knowledge is far superior to the wealth of both the earth and the heavens.

The Relationship of Preceptor and Student

The knowledge of the Upanishads, or *brahma vidya,* is terse, tough, and abstruse. Casual readers cannot understand any mantras or verses of the Upanishads without the help of a competent preceptor. The aspirants who desired to know brahma vidya were subjected to severe ordeals, austerities, and spiritual disciplines. For example, the *Kathopanishad* describes how Nachiketa was tested in various ways by his teacher, Yama, who wanted to be certain that Nachiketa deserved to have the secrets of the Upanishadic knowledge, and that it was not a mere emotional outburst or momentary desire, as is found today among modern students.

Yama offered Nachiketa all the best of the earth's objects— for example, a long life to live and the most beautiful of damsels—but Nachiketa spurned them all, knowing their transitory nature, and instead persisted in seeking to know the higher knowledge—the knowledge of the Absolute.

In the *Prashna Upanishad,* the preceptor Pippalada instructed his six disciples to practice austerities and continence for many years, and then afterwards told them, "Now, you may ask any question you like. If I know the answer, I will give it to you." In the celebrated passage of the *Chhandogya Upanishad,* it is also said that the preceptor instructed Indra and Virochana to practice spiritual disciplines for thirty-two years.

Virochana, the king of demons, could not acquire purity of mind and heart, and he went back home with the ignorant idea that the real Self was identical with the body. On the other hand, Indra, the king of gods, led the life of a brahmachari (celibate student) for seventy-three more years, and then realized the knowledge of the Self.

The relationship of student and preceptor is the highest of all relationships. No particular age is specified by the Upanishads for being a perfect aspirant or preceptor. Anyone who is endowed with spiritual virtues, either by the attainments of previous lives or through sincere efforts, learns to practice spiritual disciplines and is thus able to purify his mind and heart. Such an aspirant is qualified, whether he is young, old, man or woman.

Certainly, one can start at an older age. Old age is not a thing to be looked down upon; it has its own graces and maturity. It is considered to be like another childhood, though a childhood full of follies, because the mind of an old man becomes preoccupied. However, for those who decide to tread the path of light, age is not the barrier. Both young and old have the same divinity within them.

Physical strength and the capacity for work and pleasure are also not true criteria on this path. Atman, the real Self, remains unaffected by the changes of the body. The Upanishadic view regarding young and old is: "Thou art woman. Thou art the man. Thou art youth and Thou art the maiden, too. Thou art the old man tottering on his staff. Thou art born in diverse forms."

Human history has experienced many ups and downs in its search for truth, but mankind has not yet attained the highest stage of civilization and built a healthy society that brings about the awareness of the divine nature in its young and old. Two problems constantly plague modern society: one is the problem of old age and the other is the problem of inertia.

The Upanishads inspire and motivate aspirants by strengthening the desire to live for a hundred years, not merely to enjoy sensual pleasures, but to attain the goal of life and its purpose. If life is lived only in frustration and ignorance, without attaining the ultimate goal of life, living a full span of a hundred years is not desirable. The life that is lived for mere excitement or entertainment makes one insolvent and he or she is never safe.

A spiritual life leads one toward fearlessness and provides freedom from attachments, pains, and miseries, finally leading to emancipation. A path that helps one to grow, unfold, and realize truth makes life like a beautiful garden of Eden. Then, a human being becomes creative and educative. The Upanishads do not deprive one of enjoyments, provided one knows the way of enjoying and has the goal in front of him all the time.

Ishopanishad says, "Enjoy through renunciation." That is the only way through which our actions do not create bondage for us. All the actions that we perform can be used to deepen the delights of spirituality. The aim of external wisdom or materialistic prosperity is to enjoy life in the external world, while the knowledge of the Upanishads leads one to enjoy life in Reality, both within and without.

The Upanishads stress that realization is possible *in this lifetime* by making conscious and sincere efforts through pure intellect, good heart, and healthy body. One may gain sensual gratification in heaven, but nowhere do the Upanishads mention that heavenly realms offer the opportunity for a human being to attain enlightenment. No scripture says that Truth is attained in heaven by ignoring life on earth.

The merit that leads one to heaven is not everlasting, for it has a vanishing quality. Sensual joys and all external pleasures are short-lived and sooner or later make one exhausted. The Upanishads say, "Learn to be here and now and strive to attain the Truth in this lifetime." Life will be truly boring if it is endowed with pleasures both here and hereafter but lacks the knowledge of the real Self.

Life becomes creative, useful, and fruitful only when it moves toward Truth or perfection. On this poisonous tree of life, there are two fruits: the delight of self-existence and spiritual emancipation. Aspiring to live for a hundred years will give one ample opportunity to achieve fulfillment through the realization of the Self.

Aspiring to live for the enjoyment of sensory gratifications frustrates the human being, because of a lack of fulfillment. In such a case, one remains empty, full of fear, and insecure, and one gropes in the darkness. The Upanishads say, "Wake up, gain knowledge, and liberate yourself."

The modern world revolves faster and faster, day after day, and human beings are dazed and unable to find their bearings. Modern man finds himself deep in this situation: his past is unrecoverable, his present is uncertain, and his future is an interrogation. Never in the history of mankind has the human being ever experienced such utter darkness within himself, in the midst of such abundant prosperity outside himself.

The modern economy governs modern men and women, yet modern people are seeking for light to lead them. Their hearts are crying for Truth today, for life and health. The ancient prayer echoes silently in the hearts of modern men and women: "From the unreal, lead me to the Real, From darkness, lead me to Light, From death lead me to Immortality."

There are two thoughts that are associated with the word "salvation" or "emancipation." A taboo hounds the minds and hearts of Eastern philosophers, and that is the fear of rebirth. The joy of spirituality departs if the human being's mind is overpowered and his heart is overshadowed by fear and lack of success. Modern man thinks constantly but has not yet built a philosophy that can truly guide him. Thus, he remains without a guide, from within and without.

The philosophers of the East and West both examine the nature of the world and analyze the lifeline hung between the two points of birth and death. Religionists, too, often discuss sin and fear. Once, a sage was asked by someone, "Do you love God?" "Oh yes!" he replied. "But do you not hate the devil?" was the second question, and the sage replied, "My love for God does not spare a single moment of time to hate the devil." Similarly, St. Teresa exclaimed, "Oh, Lord, spare us from sullen saints." Socrates, Guru Nanak Dev, Kabir, and many other sages were endowed with humor and laughter.

Fear seems to have played an excessive role in the minds of some philosophers. They pray and ask for God's grace and are obsessed by the ideas of fear and rebirth. These two create negative attitudes. These negative thoughts have been digging deep in the hearts of philosophers for thousands of years. It has resulted in insensitivity toward the duties and relation-ships of the world and has made such thinkers totally unfit to pursue spiritual welfare, as well as social duties. Fear invites danger and invades the personality, thus making one a hypo-critical buffoon.

If one pursues the path of spirituality while neglecting social ethics, one cannot be content. Faiths such as Hinduism, Buddhism, and Jainism are obsessed by the idea of renunciation and ignore the essential duties that are a must in daily life. Renunciation should not be used as an escape, but as a culmination of spiritual virtues that come as a result of both spiritual practices in the external world and prayer, meditation, and contemplation in the inner world.

Upanishadic philosophy leads an aspirant to first gain inner strength. It is inner strength that expresses itself in external strength. Jesus warned his disciples, "For he that hath, to him shall be given, and he that hath not, from him shall be taken, even that which he hath."

The teachings of the Upanishads lead the aspirant to fearlessness and strength. The delight of awareness of the ultimate Existence and the value of cheerfulness in one's daily responsibilities are important in Upanishadic teachings. True freedom comes when one is free from the pressures of fear and awakens to the height of freedom and delight. True freedom comes when one knows one's own Self and is not influenced by self-created fear and misery.

Fortunate is he or she who is fearless and sees the Supreme Lord dwelling in all beings, the Imperishable in perishable things. Fear of being reborn, fear of dying, fear of losing what one has, and fear of not gaining what one desires—all these give way as fearfulness dies. Weakness and fear are two great enemies, deadlier than death. In *Julius Caesar,* Shakespeare said, "Cowards die many times before their deaths; the valiant never taste of death but once."

The vast store of human and spiritual energy lies in the Upanishadic verses that generate heroism and lead an aspirant on the path of light. It is knowledge of Truth that makes an aspirant immortal. That is the immortal Self of the human being. The more spiritual one becomes, the more fearless, gentle, and compassionate he or she becomes. Anything that makes one physically, intellectually, or spiritually weak should be seen as a stumbling block and rejected as disastrous to one's path.

The quest for Truth is strengthening, invigorating, and enlightening. Spirituality declines and degeneration begins when spiritual leaders become weak and cannot boldly teach the Truth.

A real aspirant surely will not aspire to go to heaven, for he knows that heavenly joys are short-lived, and he will become lost in sensory pleasures. These will distract him from constant awareness of the indwelling Lord. Due to an abundant exuberance of pleasures in heaven, one falls back and then again has to make an effort to walk on the path. This birth should not be wasted, either by brooding on past lives or by imagining the future pleasures of heaven.

Mundaka Upanishad

Mundaka Upanishad belongs to the *Atharva Veda* and presumably to the *Shaunakiya Sakha,* since its teachings were taught to Shaunaka by Angiras, who learned this vidya from Satyavaha-Bharadvaja, the disciple of Atharva, the eldest son and pupil of Brahma. This vidya is called *para vidya* (the knowledge of the other shore) and is also considered to be *sarva vidya pratistha,* the source of all vidyas, from which all knowledge springs.

The para vidya or the higher knowledge taught in this Upanishad removes the superimposed veil of ignorance obscuring atman, just as the razor shaves off the hair covering the head. This Upanishad is primarily intended for higher aspirants, for the attainment of the Eternal and Imperishable.

There are sixty-four verses or mantras in *Mundaka Upanishad,* which are divided into three chapters, each comprising two sections. The etymological meaning of the word *mundaka* denotes a shaving razor and a person with a shaven head, meaning a sannyasi or a monk.

The *Mundaka Upanishad* and the *Prashna Upanishad,* having their origin in the *Atharva Veda,* are complementary; what is taught in one is elaborated upon in the other. Vyasa, the compiler of the Vedas, also used the first through the sixth verses of the *Mundaka Upanishad* in composing the first aphorism of the *Vedanta Sutra.*

Like other Upanishads, *Mundaka Upanishad* takes the form of a dialogue between the preceptor and his disciple. In this case, Angiras, the preceptor, and Shaunaka, a fully prepared disciple, have a dialogue. Shaunaka humbly asks the question of the preceptor, Angiras, "Sir, what is that by knowing which, all this becomes known?" The preceptor, seeing in Shaunaka the burning desire to have the knowledge of Brahman—Absolute Truth—begins to teach him both the lower and the higher knowledge.

A SUMMARY OF THE CHAPTERS

Chapter 1: Canto 1

This canto describes the succession of teaching. Brahma, the first born, taught Atharva the knowledge of the Absolute; Atharva taught Angir, and Angir taught Satyavaha, and Satyavaha transmitted the same knowledge to Angiras. Angiras imparted the knowledge to Shaunaka, a householder from the great hall.

In the first canto, it is important to note that the knowledge of Brahman, as described in the Vedas, is called shruti, meaning, "that which has been heard by the sages in a deep state of meditation." Therefore, the shrutis, or teachings of the Vedas, are not of human origin. They are impersonal revelations.

This canto first describes two kinds of knowledge—the lower knowledge pertaining to and relating to the external world, and the higher knowledge leading to the Absolute Truth. In this canto, the nature of the imperishable Reality is also described in order to explain higher knowledge. This canto describes the evolution of the universe by saying that everything we see in this universe arises from Brahman. First is the life-force and then the mind and the *tattvas*.

Chapter 1: Canto 2

Canto 2 gives a glimpse of the sacrificial rituals performed by the householder to gain success and prosperity in the external world. It also provides a concise description of the sacrificial fire and the regulations regarding the ritual. This canto speaks of the seven tongues of fire, a concept that is better understood by the yogis—those who are fully acquainted with, and have experience of, the *chakras* (centers of energy). The result of these sacrificial ceremonies and rituals lead one to heaven.

Avidya and its offshoots are also explained. Desires and actions are not means, nor do they have the ability to lead the aspirant in attaining Absolute Truth. By performing sacrifices, rituals, and *agnihotra,* the fire ritual, one can attain heavenly joys, but those joys are short-lived and transitory. Those who practice higher knowledge attain *brahmaloka,* the realm of Brahma, which is the highest of all heavenly realms.

In this canto, it is also explained that an aspirant should be humble, have a burning desire, and be fully prepared to tread the path of light before he or she approaches the preceptor. The knowledge of Brahman or the Absolute is transmitted only to those fortunate few who are fully prepared.

Chapter 2: Canto 1

Different names and forms of the universe arise from one Brahman, like sparks from the fire. With this simile, the aspirant becomes aware that his atman is identical with Brahman.

Saguna Brahman, that is. Brahman with attributes, is also explained, as well as *nirguna* Brahman, Brahman without attributes.

In the process of evolution, the process by which a human being assumes his duties is described. Everything arises from Brahman and it is all his manifestation.

Chapter 2: Canto 2

This canto describes atman dwelling in the cave of the heart. It is like a hub that guides the movement of all the forces in human life—*prana,* mind, and senses. It provides a guideline to aspirants and leads them to meditate on the syllable *AUM,* explaining that *AUM is* the bow, the individual soul is the arrow, and Brahman is the target. The preceptor gives instructions on the path of meditation to the aspirant whose sole goal is to attain Brahman.

Chapter 3: Canto 1

This canto begins with a beautiful metaphor, which describes two birds with golden feathers. One is the individual self and the other is pure atman. They both perch on the same branch of the tree of life. One tastes the fruit, while the other only witnesses, remaining unaffected and aloof.

This canto is dedicated to inner practices and prescribes the methods of self-control and practice of truth. Importance is given to the spiritual disciplines that are essential for attaining the knowledge of Brahman. Intellect needs to be purified and sharpened before it begins to function in such a way that obstacles are not created.

This philosophy explains that the omniscient dwells everywhere, but the aspirant should learn to see that same omniscience within himself. Once he realizes his atman, or Self, he realizes the Self of all. Then he is worthy of all praise.

Chapter 3: Canto 2

All renunciates and seekers of truth are inspired by this canto. The mere study of the scriptures does not lead one to the highest knowledge. A weak person can never attain; therefore inner strength, which is based on the spiritual dimension of life, is important.

One who knows Brahman becomes Brahman. This canto describes how the illumined soul drops his body and becomes one with the Absolute Brahman. This canto is a culmination of all the practices that inspire a renunciate.

Conclusion

This Upanishad is also called *Mantra Upanishad.* The contents clearly reveal that these verses are not to be used as invocations, prayers, or in sacrificial rituals. These mantras have beauty in meter and diction, and are both exalted in their spiritual beauty and uniform in their sublimity.

This Upanishad may be considered a practical guide for both householders and renunciates. All mantras in their pristine purity are mastered by long contemplation and constant meditation, and by diving deep into their inner significance, which surely inspires a student to tread the path of knowledge toward the Absolute. Every word of this Upanishad breathes practical knowledge, which helps the aspirant to realize the supreme Truth.

Peace Invocation

AUM! May our ears hear that which is auspicious. May we see that which is auspicious. May we sing the praise of the Lord and live a fully-allotted span of life, with perfect health and strength. May glorious Indra and Pushan, the knower of all, bring auspiciousness. May Tarksya, who protects us from all harm, and Brihaspati, the great fountain of wisdom, bring goodness and auspiciousness into our lives. AUM!
Shantih, shantih, shantih.

Peace is a state of equanimity and tranquility, which the aspirant can attain by understanding his own mind and its modifications, and most importantly, by establishing harmony among the various modifications of the mind—*manas* (lower mind), *chitta* (the reservoir of knowledge within), *buddhi* (higher mind), and *ahamkara* (sense of I-ness). When all human efforts are exhausted, the student despairs and begins to pray.

During the Upanishadic period, preceptors and pupils prayed together so that they could establish harmony in their relationship, and so that the subject matter could be understood in a congenial atmosphere with clear communication. It is true that prayer can answer those questions that are not answered by anyone on earth, provided the prayer is conducted with one-pointedness and perfect humility. This invocation also teaches the aspirant to understand the functioning of the senses, which constantly dissipate and distort the energy of the mind.

The gods mentioned in the invocation refer to the finest forces dwelling in the human being, such as the first unit of life (prana) and the dormant energy *(kundalini).* So these gods are not ultimate Truth but merely the forces that help the wheel of life to rotate around its hub—*paramatman* or Absolute Truth. Prayer purifies the way of the soul, but knowledge of the Self alone dispels the darkness of ignorance.

"*Aum!* May our ears hear that which is auspicious." This means that an aspirant should learn to hear only the scriptures or those sayings that are not distracting or dissipating to the mind.

"May we see that which is auspicious," also means to learn not to create obstacles by dissipating the mind through our eyes.

"May we sing the praise of the Lord and live a fully- allot-ted span of life, with perfect health and strength." The aspirant should remember that the invocation or prayer is not addressed to the Lord of the universe. The aspirant cannot conceive or grasp this in full, but from the very beginning, he or she should learn to take his or her own body as a shrine and the inner dweller, atman, as the ultimate *deva* (bright being). But before one attains the knowledge of atman, which is identical to the Absolute and without a second, he or she has to become aware of the finer forces of life, which are called "gods." This subject matter is understood only by those aspirants who practice the internal path.

The aspirants who are successful in conducting their

prayers in this way are successful in understanding the knowledge imparted by the preceptor, because the Upanishadic sayings are terse, tough, and abstruse. Therefore, by the grace of the Self, the Self is known.

At the end of the invocation, *"Aum, Shantih, Shantih, Shantih,"* the word *shantih* (peace) is repeated three times. *Aum,* the cosmic sound, which expands itself into all the alphabets of the world, is the highest of symbols according to Upanishadic literature. Further discussion will elaborate on this sacred syllable. We need peace on all dimensions—the physical, mental, and spiritual. That is why, at the end of the invocation, the word *shantih* is repeated three times.

Chapter

1

Mundaka Upanishad

CANTO 1

VERSE 1:

> **Aum!** *Brahma, as the first manifested one, the*
> *designer, architect, and guardian of the universe,*
> *taught his eldest son, Atharva, the sovereign*
> *science of Brahman, the foundation of all sciences.*

The first born, who is the creator and protector of the universe, is Brahma. Brahma manifests all the forms of the world directly, and Brahma is the first manifested being, rising from the unmanifest. Absolute Truth. The student should be aware that there are three words that sound similar—*Brahman, Brahma,* and *brahmana.*

Brahman is the Absolute Truth, One without a second. Brahma is the first born. Brahmana is the knower of Brahman, or the custodian of the scriptures pertaining to the knowledge of Brahman or the Vedas.

VERSE 2:

> *The science of ultimate Truth was that which*
> *Brahma taught to his eldest son, Atharva, who*
> *transmitted that knowledge to Angir first. Later,*
> *Angir taught it to Satyavaha-Bharadvaja, and*
> *Satyavaha transmitted it in succession to Angir as.*

Brahma is the creator in the Vedic trinity. Therefore, Brahma is not the same as the impersonal Absolute. He is considered to be the first knower of Brahman, Absolute Truth. This knowledge was orally transmitted by Brahma to his eldest son Atharva. In ancient times, the science of Brahman, the cosmic spirit, was then imparted to Angir, who passed it on to Satyavaha-Bharadvaja. Thus, the science of supreme knowledge descended from the great sages, and this unbroken tradition is called the *guru lineage.*

VERSE 3:

> *Shaunaka, the great householder, approached*
> *Angiras in a proper manner and asked: "Upon*
> *knowing what, sir, does all become known?"*

It is to be understood that the tradition of sharing knowledge, both higher and lower (spiritual knowledge and knowledge of the world) is important and essential in the history of human growth. These days, young people do not enjoy sharing in this delight. Thus, they are deprived of the knowledge that comes from older people.

It is experience that leads, and when we learn to examine our experiences, we find that there are very few experiences that lead or guide human beings at the time of difficulty. This also means that an aspirant should develop the inclination to listen to older people and be benefitted by their experience.

VERSE 4:

> *There are two aspects of knowledge to be attained—the knowers of Brahman tell us that. They are the higher knowledge and the lower knowledge.*

The great householder, Shaunaka, coming from the great hall, humbly approaches Angiras and asks the question, "Sir, what is that knowledge by which everything in the world becomes known?" The question itself makes evident that the knowledge of the *Mundaka Upanishad* was finally transmitted by the sage Angiras to his favorite disciple Shaunaka, who was a householder rather than a monk. Therefore, it is clear that the contents of the *Mundaka Upanishad* are equally revered and meant to be practiced by both renunciates and householders.

Angiras describes these teachings: There are two aspects of knowledge to be attained. The knowers of the Vedas say that one is called *para vidya*, the knowledge of the beyond, and the other is called *apara vidya,* the knowledge of the external world. Life is like a stream flowing from eternity to eternity. It cannot be perceived in a comprehensive mariner unless we have the profound knowledge of both shores. "This shore" means the world, and "the other shore" means the knowledge of the Absolute.

Many of us do not become aware of the knowledge of the beyond, which is the very foundation of all aspects of any other knowledge. The knowledge of the Absolute Truth is the foundation of all sciences. The knowledge of this shore also has its importance. It helps one to know the mind and its various functions, as well as to understand actions and the way they should be performed, and the function of speech and the manner in which it should be utilized.

This knowledge makes one successful and prosperous in the external world, but without gaining the profound knowledge of the Truth of truths, which is the subtlest among all levels of life, one does not remain content. Contentment is the greatest of all wealths that one can have. Those who are dedicated to the path of contemplation and meditation on the Absolute Brahman say this.

VERSE 5:

> *Of these, the lower science is composed of the* **Rig,**
> **Yajur, Sama,** *and* **Atharva Vedas,** *phonetics, ritual,*
> *grammar, etymology, poetics, and astronomy. The*
> *higher science is that by which the immutable,*
> *Eternal Truth is made known.*

The lower knowledge consists of the study of the *Rig, Yajur, Sama,* and *Atharva Vedas,* phonetics, the rules of rituals to be performed by a human being, grammar, etymology, poetics, and astronomy.

The higher knowledge is that by which the knowledge of Brahman or the Imperishable Reality is attained. Just as trichotomy does not oppose dichotomy, similarly, the higher knowledge does not oppose lower knowledge. During ancient times, human beings were prosperous in the world and at the same time, made an effort to attain Brahman with all the means they had available to them.

There are two sides to this issue: Can lower knowledge help one to attain Brahman? Can worldly prosperity be made a means to attain Brahman, or is lower knowledge gained to know the transitory nature of the objects of the world? Lower knowledge actually means that the aspirant earns the means to facilitate his or her search and to create favorable circumstances for prayer, meditation, and contemplation, which are the real means to attain final liberation or realize Absolute Truth.

Lower knowledge, of course, does not directly help the aspirant to attain final emancipation, but if lower knowledge is not gained, it creates obstacles for the aspirant. Therefore, in a holistic approach toward life, one can learn something from the lower knowledge. Yet without the higher knowledge, lower knowledge will distort the human mind and dissipate human potential. Of course, the goal is to attain the higher knowledge, which directly helps one to liberate himself from all bondage.

VERSE 6:

> *That which is invisible, ungraspable, without origin, that transcends all, having no eyes and no ears, that which is without hands and feet; eternal, all-pervading, present in all, very subtle, that unchangeable Truth is the origin of beings, whom the wise men see.*

Real power resides within, with all its potentials. The external world is a mere expression of the power residing within. It is beyond sense perception and even beyond the ability of the mind to conceptualize. A mind can be trained to have lower knowledge and to not allow obstacles on the path of enlightenment, but the mind itself has no power to lead one to the knowledge of the Absolute.

Higher knowledge is invisible, beyond the reach of the senses and mind. Therefore, it cannot be grasped. The higher knowledge is the origin of all the branches of knowledge. It was never born; therefore, it has no attributes. It has no eyes, ears, hands, or feet. That which is limitless and cannot be measured, which is the subtlest of the subtle, is not describable.

The wise seers in their deep meditation, after establishing tranquility, perceived this knowledge, or rather, this revelation came to them from the source of all creation. With the following simile, you will understand more clearly: Just as the seed of a tree contains all the potentials and qualities of the tree, including its roots, trunk, branches, leaves, flowers, and fruits, so, too, do we find that all this—here, there, and everywhere, mobile and immobile—has risen from the Absolute Brahman.

The wise, therefore, choose to pursue the knowledge of Brahman, the indestructible and immeasurable Absolute. The first half of this mantra explains Brahman by the negation of attributes. But the second half of the mantra explains the Absolute Truth by using certain positive adjectives. The attributeless Brahman is the single, self-existent Reality in all the forms of the world but is Itself unaffected and uninfluenced by them.

VERSE 7:

> *Just as a spider releases and reels in its web, just*
> *as the herbs (all trees and plants) emerge from*
> *the earth, or just as the hair grows out of the*
> *human body, so does the universe emerge from*
> *(and become reabsorbed into) the indestructible,*
> *Absolute Truth.*

In this verse, simple illustrations are given to explain Brahman as the *summum bonum* of all beings. Brahman is the source of all beings. Just as the spider projects a web through producing thread and then draws in its thread again, so also does Brahman, the real cause, bring forth this universe and draw it in again. Bringing forth is called creation, and withdrawing is called dissolution. Just as plants grow spontaneously and effortlessly on the earth, so, too, in a similar manner, does this universe of ours grow from its source, the one Absolute Brahman.

Brahman does not need any support or the help of any other entity or cause. As the thread of a spider is not different from or unrelated to the spider's body, so the universe is not different from Brahman. The plants, trees, and shrubs are not different from the earth. The hair is not different from a man's head. Shaving the head is a painless experience, for hair is completely inert, although it grows out of a living head. Just as hair grows effortlessly from the human body, without creating stress, so, too, from Brahman, the source of intelligence and brilliance itself, does this inert universe emanate.

In the first simile, Brahman is described as the very basis for the creation and dissolution of the entire universe. The second simile expresses that even after manifestation of this universe, it rests in Brahman alone, for this universe of ours is completely dependent on Brahman. The third simile asserts that manifestation occurs without stressful effort.

It is interesting to note here that the manifestation of the universe is not the transformation of the Absolute, but only its projection. Therefore, Brahman is both the material and efficient cause of the universe. The spontaneous nature of manifestation has been explained with simple illustrations. Brahman, without any extraneous support or cause, projects this universe, and finally the universe merges back into Brahman.

VERSE 8:

> *Brahman manifests through* tapas *(knowledge).*
> *From that evolves* annam, *the essence of nourish-*
> *ment. From that evolves prana (life force), the*
> *mind, and the five gross elements (earth, water,*
> *fire, air, and space), the law of karma, and the*
> *inevitable fruit of karma, which cannot be avoided.*

Brahman, with the thought of delight, manifested this universe. It is important to note here that the word *tapes* has different meanings when used in various scriptures or contexts. Here, *tapas* means "profound and delightful knowledge." According to Patanjali, the codifier of yoga science, tapas means learning to control the mind by directing the energy dissipated through the senses. That discipline which helps the aspirant to direct the senses in an orderly manner is tapas.

An aspirant has to make an effort, but for Brahman, this process is spontaneous, effortless, and a matter of delight. By using his own knowledge. Brahman manifested this world, and as in mathematics, One becomes many. Take any digit, for instance: the existence of that digit depends on the unit one. Without one, the digit will lose its value; even the zeros have validity only if they are used after the digit one.

This means that mathematics, the positive science that is the very basis of all modern sciences, uses "one" first, and all subsequent numbers are actually only repetitions and additions of one. Therefore, there is only One Absolute, self-existent Truth and that, in its own delight and will, became many.

Food grows on the earth. The earth was projected by means of tapas, which helps to sustain life on this earth and constantly supplies pranic energy to that unit of energy which is the subtlest in the human body. One can say that it is the first unit of the life force that projects mind, prana, and then the elements, since from food comes energy, and then mind.

It is true that without food, the mind cannot function, and without the functions of the mind, no one can perform actions. When one starts performing actions, he gets entangled and creates a whirlpool of karma for himself. Because of their lack of skill, people create misery and bondage for themselves.

Commonly, the word *tapas* implies heat and thought, but Western philosophers sometimes translate tapas as "brooding." When tapas is used in relation to Brahman, tapas is knowledge that projects itself into the universe that is called "the manifested universe." The word *annam* also means food. That signifies that one should learn to enjoy the food one eats with the spirit of joy for the sake of maintaining good health, so that the body becomes a useful instrument.

Prana has diverse meanings: it is the first unit of life, energy, the "vital breath," or as described in the Upanishads, the "first ray of manifestation." Here, the word is literally used to mean the "golden egg," *Hiranyagarbha,* which is the central powerhouse that diversifies manifestation. Hindu religionists call the creator-God of the Hindu trinity Brahma, or Hiranyagarbha. This verse also provides a description of the five great elements that constitute the physical world.

Work and action, with reference to the physical world, are related to the enjoyment of the fruits of those actions, which creates an endless chain. The aspirant, after attaining the knowledge of the Absolute, gains freedom from this entanglement. The aspirant should remember that this mantra refers to saguna Brahman—Brahman with attributes.

According to the Hindu trinity, there are three aspects of manifestation—the abilities to create, preserve, and dissolve. The governing forces of these three are called Brahma, Visnu, and Mahesha, respectively. But Absolute, self-existent Truth, or Brahman, remains unchanged and unaffected by its manifestation or projection.

When the universe comes into manifestation, the Absolute Truth is known as Brahman with attributes— saguna Brahman. Because of the names and forms of this universe, it may look different and seem to be a separate entity but in reality, the whole manifestation is the illusory superimposition of various names and forms. It is because of the cosmic veil that we see many in One.

This cosmic veil, maya, has no self-existent reality. It depends on Brahman, Absolute Truth. Rather, one can say that it is one of the forces of Brahman through which the universe is manifested. We will describe maya at length so that aspirants do not become confused, for it is maya that has created all confusions.

It is important to understand that the Upanishadic literature describes manifestation and non-manifestation in two ways: 1) the process through which things are seen in their tangible form and 2) the "seeds" of those forms. These two states are called "the day and night of Brahma." The period of manifestation is termed a *kalpa* or cycle.

Whenever or wherever the words *creation* and *manifestation* are used, they refer to the beginning of a cycle. A new cycle begins by the will of *Ishvara* or saguna Brahman. But it should be remembered that a cycle's character is determined by the accumulated actions or samskaras of the living beings of the previous cycle.

Mere matter, therefore, is not able to manifest the world. Consciousness, intelligence, and matter united make the universe. The universe full of attributes is perceived as it is because of maya.

VERSE 9:

*From Him (Absolute Truth) which includes all
knowledge and omniscience, and whose discipline
and practice are made up of knowledge, comes the
immanent form of Brahman, Hiranyagarbha, and
the principles of name, color, and substance.*

The first born, Brahma, Ishvara, or Hiranyagarbha, and the
individual souls—including all creatures and all the nutrients
that nourish the creatures—rise from only One, Who is wise
and omniscient and whose creative thought is knowledge. The
aspirant should clearly understand how the Sanskrit terms are
used, because such distinctions in meaning are important.

Saguna Brahman, or the cosmos (Brahman with attributes),
in relation to maya, surveys the whole universe in its totality.
The creative thought is essentially knowledge. Brahman's force
of will is entirely different and unlike what we consider to be the
creative genius of beings on earth. To be creative in the world
means to create something new with materials at hand, such
as building a table out of wood. *Jiva*, the individual soul, associated with avidya (ignorance), has limitations, but Brahman
is limitless. Additionally, because of his association with ignorance, an individual soul or aspirant has to make efforts, and
do tapas, or austerities, to regain his original dignity or prestige
and to reestablish himself in his essential nature.

While this effort is called tapas, in the case of Absolute Brahman, tapas is spontaneous and effortless, because Brahman is
not affected by maya. This same maya is one of the powers of
Brahman, which becomes known as avidya when it involves the
individual and his entanglement with the law of karma (action).
Then, one is caught by the snare of avidya. That is why he has

to make these sincere efforts. Human effort is always human, but the knowledge one uses to make effort is always divine. Any sincere effort made by an aspirant with knowledge will help him to break the fetters of avidya and become free from the bondage created by it.

Jiva is endowed with all the same qualities of Brahman, but jiva, through its association with avidya, thinks itself to be limited. Here, the aspirant should understand that there is a vast difference between human creation and divine creation. Human creation is dependent on the existence of something different and separate from the doer. However, in relation to Brahman's creation. Brahman does not have to depend on any other force to manifest the universe. When the jiva, the individual soul, learns to be free from the strong clutches of avidya, he realizes his true Self and becomes one with Brahman.

The Upanishad gives a subtle definition of cosmic ignorance and avidya. To be creative in the world is to be precise and mechanistic, yet as far as the spiritual interpretation is concerned, to be creative in relation to Brahman is spontaneous and effortless.

The student should understand that human effort to attain divine consciousness is very important. He should not take it for granted that he will one day spontaneously realize the Absolute Truth without doing tapas. Tapas is that discipline that helps one to grow, unfold, and purify the way of the soul. The discipline should not be imposed, but accepted by the aspirant as a matter of spiritual delight.

Here ends the first canto of Chapter 1.

chapter 1

CANTO 2

VERSE 1:

> *The ritualistic ceremonies, which were revealed to
> the seers, were described in many ways in the three
> Vedas—Rig, Yajur, and Sama Veda. Those being
> desirous to attain their meritorious results practice
> them. This is your path leading toward virtuous ends.*

It is true that the sacred hymns of the Vedas are related to
ritualistic works. They are treated and described elaborately in
three of the Vedas. Those who are desirous to gain these results
attain prosperity and joy in this world and hereafter.

In the *Rig, Yajur,* and *Sama Vedas,* the priests who perform
the fire ceremony are called *hota, udgata,* and *addhvaryu.* The
presence of the brahmana, who is well-versed in the *Atharva
Veda,* is also important. He remains present during the period
of the ceremony.

Atharva Veda does not contain any rules or regulations for
the fire ceremony (agnihotra). In the *satya* and *treta yugas,* the

first two cycles of the universe, aspirants only practiced tapas, contemplation, and meditation. In the beginning, when the world was manifested, human beings did not have any necessity at all to attain worldly prosperity and remained in contemplation and meditation all the time. Actually, the rituals started in *dvapara,* the third cycle.

These ceremonies were performed according to the injunctions and rules laid down by the Vedas and always produced definite results if performed according to the Vedic injunctions. Actually, there is a yogic explanation for this ceremony. Five elements, five subtle senses, five gross senses, two pranas (inhalation and exhalation, *prana* and *apana),* and higher buddhi, or pure intellect, with her lord *jivatman,* are like the eighteen rishis (seers), and they are performing *yajna* (worship or sacrifice) in the city of life all the time.

Into the fire of life the oblations are constantly offered, and this is really the true explanation of the word *agnihotra.* Here, it is useful to note that there are more than three hundred meanings of the word *agni,* or fire, but of these, about forty are most important and prominent.

Agni means a Brahmin, a man of wisdom; agni means the fire of light; agni means the life breath; agni means prana; agni means heat; agni also means leader. The meaning depends on where the word is applied. During that highly sophisticated and brilliant age, satya yuga, the rishis endowed with all the virtues knew the way of maintaining perfect health on all levels—physical, mental, and spiritual. Any yajna or ceremony that was performed was related to life either directly or indirectly.

When we say a human being should learn to perform his karma or action skillfully, this is a modern way of explaining that any karma performed skillfully bears desired fruits for the doer. Here the aspirant sacrifices his lower nature, the ignorant nature that is enveloped by avidya, to the fire of knowledge.

It is true that a human being is a compound of three qualities—the animal aspect within him, the human in him, and the divine aspect in him. In the *Bhagavad Gita,* these aspects are referred to as *tamas, rajas,* and *sattva.* When an aspirant learns to tame the animal within and expresses his creative, human potential through mind, action, and speech, then he becomes fully civilized and is prepared to attain divinity. The divine qualities in the human being remain latent as long as the human and animal qualities remain predominant.

The concepts of tamas, rajas, and sattva are also known as the three *gunas,* or the three principles that combine in various ways to make up apparent reality. Tamas is the obscuring or veiling quality, associated with darkness, ignorance, inertia, and doubt. Tamas is heavy, slow-moving, and dense and has the most concrete material quality. It also has the traits of stability or permanence. The most tamasic aspect of the human being is the body.

Rajas is the energizing quality associated with movement, desire, and action. It is a more dynamic quality than tamas, but it can also be considered to be agitated or restless. Its most useful aspect is the potential to direct energy in a specific manner. All human activities are related to this guna, especially all creative activities. This quality leads one to earn, to have, and to enjoy the things of the world. Those who are led by the predominance of this particular quality remain active in the external world. The most rajasic aspect of the human being is the mind.

Sattva, by contrast, is the quality associated with energy that is balanced, serene, harmonious, and highly evolved. It is associated with clarity, brightness, and wisdom. The sattvic aspect of the human being is atman, or the spirit within.

On the individual human level, the aspirant needs to understand and learn to balance the tendencies of the three gunas—learning to wisely channel the tamasic (or animal) and the rajasic (or human) tendencies, as well as to cultivate that which is sattvic or eternal within. Once this sattvic aspect is cultivated, it becomes easy for the aspirant to see things as they are. Then, the mind remains one-pointed and peaceful, and does not become agitated by the tribulations of life.

It is important for the aspirant to become sattvic on all levels. For example, eating sattvic food means to avoid eating foods that create inertia or sloth or that, on the other hand, create excessive stimulation in the aspirant's sexual system or distortions in the expression of sexuality. The foods that agitate the human sexual tendencies are actually quite injurious, because excessive sexual activity does tax the nervous system and eventually, can even lead to mental degeneration and emotional disorientation.

A regulated sexual life is very important for a householder so that he is undisturbed by the tendency of the mind to constantly travel to the sexual groove that has been created in the mind through engaging in constant thoughts about sex. It is important that the aspirant not go to extremes—either thinking of sex constantly and being sexually obsessed in his behavior, or thinking too much about sex, and yet not doing sex at all. This is a false restraint or suppression that is unhealthy and leads to a kind of passivity. Thus, it is important to develop control over the four primitive fountains—food, sex, sleep, and self-preservation.

Poor food habits can lead one to excessive sleep and to suffering from extended nightmares, which is injurious to one's health. If one repeatedly sleeps more than is necessary, this pattern can lead to the habit of inertia. It is difficult to break such a habit pattern because the human personality itself is composed of habit patterns. Therefore, the beginner should learn to regulate these four aspects of behavior by carefully observing his or her own capacity.

To become increasingly sattvic always means creating a balance in human life, rather than acting in the extreme. When an aspirant learns to sit still and establishes serenity in the breath, then he has to face his mind. If he has deepened the sexual groove in his mind by constantly thinking those thoughts, then they come forward and disturb him in his meditation. Food and the actions we perform in the world do affect the mind equally as much as our thoughts create distortions in our external behavior. Both these aspects—mind and behavior—have the capacity to affect each other. In the sattvic mind there is always clarity and decisiveness and the faculty of buddhi functions accurately.

Renunciates do not waste time thinking about food, sex, sleep, or self-preservation, because they have already either found the way to develop control over these appetites or have learned the method of sublimation. There are certain *yogic kriyas* that they use to attain control over their sexual urges.

However, for householders, it is more useful if they learn how to direct their energies by eating a healthy, balanced diet, doing sex in a balanced way, moderating their sleep needs, and refusing to entertain thoughts of a fearful nature, which threaten the very fabric of their internal states. In either case, to be successful in life one should learn to tame the tamasic tendencies in himself, which make him violent, insensitive, and unjust.

One becomes increasingly sattvic by curtailing the performance of useless actions that steal the purity of his character.

One also seeks to avoid negative thoughts that deprive him of clarity of mind and rob his mind of cheerfulness. Wise are those who gradually watch and control their own internal tendencies, inclinations, and desires, and who do not allow their minds to wander in the grooves of sexuality or any other activities performed in daily life that are injurious for their growth.

One can sit quietly for some time and analyze his own thought process. If one does not allow injurious thoughts to be materialized, and if helpful and beneficial thoughts are encouraged, the mind also forms a particular habit. Finally a time comes when tamasic thoughts no longer arise, when rajasic thoughts arise only under control, and sattvic thoughts become predominant. Such a sattvic mind can contemplate, meditate, and pray successfully.

This verse also clearly indicates that a householder's life, the second rung of the ladder of life, is only a preparation to attain the higher rungs. Developing gradually this attitude of self-observation and self-discipline does not become hard on a householder if self-control is willfully practiced rather than imposed by the force of social values or external authority.

In the previous canto, the sage Angiras imparted both the higher and lower knowledge to Shaunaka. It is with the help of the lower knowledge that one becomes prosperous and with the help of higher knowledge that one attains moksha—liberation.

Imparting the knowledge of the para vidya (Absolute Truth) to Shaunaka indicates that householders should understand that this step, though important, is still preparatory to attaining the higher rungs. This comforts householders; they understand that all the activities and duties they perform during their lives are necessary as means to prevent obstacles from arising on their path. Many people think that they are "merely householders," and that the knowledge of the Absolute can be imparted only to renunciates, which is absolutely incorrect.

The *Kathopanishad* says, "*Uttisthita jagrata prapya varan nivodhata*—Wake up, gain knowledge, and attain the Absolute Truth, which is the fate of all human beings." Therefore, the sayings of the Upanishads are shared by those who tread the path of renunciation and also by those who tread the path of selfless action.

The word *samsara* means "that which continues without beginning or end." Actions, means, and results are three characteristics of this world. Those who become attached to the joys and objects of the world—which are constantly changing—remain miserable, and those who are free from the rounds of birth, growth, death, and decay attain salvation. To attain self-realization, one attains freedom on all levels.

This canto deals with the description of lower knowledge. The way of performing meritorious actions and enjoying their fruits comes within the range of lower knowledge. When aspirants analyze the fruits received through their actions, then they understand the importance of cultivating the higher knowledge, which leads them to final liberation.

VERSE 2:

> *When the fire is ablaze, an aspirant should offer*
> *the oblations systematically, one by one, in the*
> *prescribed manner.*

The second mantra has a deep significance. It is true that for all ceremonies, deeds, and actions, the fire of life is essential, so the Vedas speak of fire and the fire ceremony, which is akin to the life force and is the first and foremost ceremony. Without it, nothing can be done in the world. This mantra speaks of the lighting of the fire with the flames that sparkle, and of offering oblations of butter into the space created by the flames.

The discussion that follows explains this mantra in the light of *Tantra Shastra.* The word *tantra* means "way of," and there are three schools of Tantra—*Kaula, Mishra,* and *Samaya.* The serious aspirant should note that there are other scriptures that are considered to be auxiliary to the sayings of the Upani-shads, called the *Prayoga Shastras.* The Upanishads are the most important of the scriptures and are expressed in a methodical and concise way. They are like curriculums intended for the teacher to explain and transmit to the student. A student should learn to understand himself on all levels by studying anatomy, physiology, diet and nutrition, and the science of breath. Breath is the vehicle through which prana is supplied to the various realms of the city of life—the body, the senses and their func-tioning, both gross and subtle, and the mind and its various modifications. The student should understand the individual soul and its relationship to body, senses, and mind.

He should also learn to understand the various functions of the mind. At this stage, however, the individual soul, from which the power emanates, remains hidden from the view of a beginner. But an aspirant begins to realize that he is not the body alone, although the body certainly exists as a gross instru-ment. It is important that the body be cared for, but if one con-tinues caring for the body alone, without understanding the other deeper dimensions of life, such as the breath and the con-scious and unconscious minds, he will suffer. His ignorance and lack of awareness of the subtler and finer dimensions of life will cause pain and difficulty. The more that one knows about him-self, the more one understands the value of life.

The Tantra Shastras are helpful in learning to understand many yogic practices so long as they are not mistaken for mere sexual acts, the way they often are in the West. The purpose of the yogic science is to awaken the dormant force—the sleeping force called kundalini—and to establish *sushumna* ("the joyous mind"), so that the mind spontaneously becomes inwardly one-pointed and remains in a state of indescribable joy.

The knowledge of the seven chakras is essential. "Chakra" means wheel, as in a wheel of fortune[1].1 In the subtlemost body of the human being, which dwells in the unconscious, there are seven main chakras or focal points for the meditator.

From *muladhara chakra* at the base of the spine to *sahasrara chakra* at the crown of the head, the *anahata chakra* divides the upper hemisphere from the lower hemisphere. The upper hemisphere includes the *vishuddha, ajna,* and *sahasrara chakras*, while the lower hemisphere includes the *muladhara, svadhisthana,* and *manipura chakras.* Because anahata is the dividing line, it is used by the meditator to establish tranquility in his emotional life.

According to the Kaula school, muladhara chakra—the root chakra—is the base of the ceremony. In this ceremony, two principles of the universe—the female and the male, *shakti* and *shiva*—meet and perform the worship. These two principles were traditionally represented by a man and woman, who assumed the qualities of shiva and shakti. It was a physical union; the sexual act was performed as a worship, and would help men and women to deepen the practice of meditation. They would both light the fire of physical unity and offer the oblation of semen at the right occasion, when the fire was well-lit, with all its vigor. There

---

[1] For a further description of the system of the chakras, please study *Yoga and Psychotherapy* by Swami Rama, Rudolph Ballentine, M.D., and Swami Ajaya, Ph.D.

are many impediments which should be overcome before this ceremony is performed. When this ceremony is not performed rightly, much harm can occur to the performers.

We often find that sexual dissatisfaction leads a human being to a state of depression. According to the Kaula school, the man and woman both receive an education in learning to deal with the sexual urge, so that there is no frustration or dissatisfaction in their sexual behavior. This helps them to be free from the diseases and difficulties that arise from problems with the sexual urge. Moreover, this sexual activity is not considered to be a mere physical activity motivated only by the desire for sensory pleasure, but rather, a union between two higher principles. That awareness is constantly maintained so that this activity becomes a sort of worship.

The Mishra school chooses as the site of the worship the anahata chakra, which divides the upper hemisphere from the lower. This group performs this ceremony as *manas puja* (mental puja)—like *panchopachara puja* and *shodashopachara puja.* It is called Mishra because this particular school believes that the worship should not be only external; it also has its inner significance. Thus, the Mishra group worships internally, making the anahata chakra their focal point. Anahata chakra, which is related to the emotional life, needs to be well understood and this experience must be coordinated on the higher levels so that ecstasy is attained. It is true that through ecstasy the aspirant can attain higher knowledge effortlessly.

The third school is Samaya. The Samaya path is the highest of all paths, and is purely yogic. On this path worship is performed only internally, in the sahasrara chakra. The aspirants of this school do not perform any ceremony externally, but they do the ceremony only in a purely mental and yogic sense. That is why it is called internal worship, in which the methods of *pranayama,* meditation, and contemplation are involved. After undergoing a series of preliminary purificatory disciplines, highly evolved adepts worship the union of shiva and *parvati* (shakti), visualizing their inseparable unity at sahasrara chakra. There is nothing external in the practice. Such worship leads the aspirants to a state of *sahaja samadhi*— the state of jivanmukti. This is considered to be the highest of all the schools and is practiced by yogis and renunciates. Samaya is the rarest of all the paths of Tantra.

It is important to emphasize here that in the West, the path of Tantra is taken to mean engaging in the sexual act, but it is a ridiculous misunderstanding to say that Tantra is sex. The explanations given above are true, but householders are taught the agnihotra ceremony, called *bahiranga upasana.* These ceremonies are performed according to the rules and injunctions laid down in the Vedas. According to karma kanda, these ceremonies lead the householder to virtuous ends and it is true that when such ceremonies are correctly performed, those doing so receive positive results.

VERSE 3:

> *If the aspirant's agnihotra ceremony is not performed*
> *in the right manner, without regard to the new and*
> *full moons, the four months of the rainy season, the*
> *summer solstice, the presence of guests, the vaisvadeva*
> *ceremony, or if not performed in the prescribed*
> *manner, then it destroys the intended goal, which may*
> *stretch across all of his seven worlds.*

The third verse mentions the importance of the correct circumstances in order to perform this ritual or worship. Such a ceremony is celebrated on the day of the full moon. Four months of the rainy season, *chaturmasa,* are devoted to this ceremony. The verse says that if the performer of this ceremony does not learn to communicate with the external forces, and if the ceremony is not performed at the right time, or if the guests who witness the ceremony are not treated well, then it disturbs all seven spheres in the human body. This means that it disturbs even the deeper energy levels of the chakras.

The different sacrifices or ceremonies mentioned in this mantra are ancillary to the main ritual, called the fire ceremony. The householders, practicing the path of lower knowledge—the knowledge of the world—perform this ceremony in the external world in a literal manner.

VERSE 4:

> *These are the names of the seven tongues of fire:*
> **kali, karali, monojava, sulohita, sudhumravarna, sphulingini,** *and* **vishvaruci**—*these seven flickering flames create the seven tongues of the fire.*

It is interesting to note that the Vedic rishis clearly visualized seven colors and also had the knowledge of the seven keynotes, which are used in music all over the world. In reality, the seven colors are the basic colors, and by mixing one with the other, we can have many additional colors. This verse has a name for all seven colors or flames that arise during the ceremony from a sacrificial fire that is well-lit.

The yogis say that when the primal fire—kundalini—is awakened, it is like a serpent fire, and then one can clearly visualize all seven flames of the fire accurately. The verse says that the flames should be shining and free from smoke. No worship should be conducted unless the kundalini fire awakens fully. At the base of the spinal column, there is a cavity which is called the *kunda,* and in this kunda resides the primal fire of kundalini.

Kundalini is presently in a dormant form. With the help of the recitation of mantras, the ashes that cover the primal fire are blown off and the fire is ignited. Those who perform internal worship, who visualize and experience all seven tongues, then visualize and experience the awakening of this primal fire. These seven tongues of fire swallow the oblation offered to them; this means that all the impurities and samskaras are burned by the flames arising from the serpent-like fire that has been awakened.

VERSE 5:

> *The light of the sun's rays leads an aspirant, who*
> *performs this offering into the fire at the right time,*
> *to realize the sole sovereign of all bright beings.*

This verse provides guidelines for performing the fire ceremony for those householders who are not renunciates and do not understand the significance of yogic internal worship or yogic practices. The fire ceremony must be performed accurately, according to the rules and regulations laid down by the Vedas. The oblations that are offered should be made when the flames of the fire are fully lit. These references to oblations or worship of the fire mean "treading the path of fire."

The oblation is made of ghee (clarified butter), which signifies that one should attain the means to make the fire of light blaze to the last breath of life. Clarified butter is a purified and more refined modification of milk, and it is prepared by churning milk. When the aspirant starts to "churn" all the knowledge he has, then he uses his determination with a one-pointed long-ing to attain Brahman. The butter symbolizes this one-pointed, determined longing.

There is another important point to note: as long as smoke exists, the fire is not yet fully ablaze, and oblations are not offered. One should learn to live a life that creates only light, rather than one that creates smoke.

Actually, there are only two paths—the path of good and the path of evil—the path of light and the path of darkness. Those who follow the path of good attain prosperity in the world of objects; those who follow the path of darkness suffer on account of their ignorance. We also learn from this verse that in the external world we need to learn to discriminate the path of the pleasant from the path of good. That which is pleas-ant is not necessarily good, and that which is good may not be apparently pleasant. When the aspirant is aware of his goal in life, he chooses to follow the path of good in the external world, which is actually the first rung on the ladder of enlightenment, This is a preparation that helps an aspirant to attain the next step, which will lead him to the spiritual dimension of his life.

The verse indicates that the path of good leads the aspirant through the path of solar fire. In our solar system, there is only one sun. Although there are millions of suns in the universe, the verse says: "The sun that shines is an example that is to be followed. The sun shines and remains apart from and above all." The aspirant should do good by doing selfless actions in the world and by learning to remain unattached and unaffected all the time. This will give him the first freedom, which is freedom from the bondage of karma.

The eighteenth mantra of the *Ishopanishad* explains this: "Agni, lead me by the good path to the fruits of my actions."

VERSE 6:

> *The luminous oblations say to the performer,*
> *"Come hither, come higher, " and lead him through*
> *the rays of the sun, honoring him and greeting him*
> *delightfully and pleasantly. This is the holy heaven*
> *of Brahma, attained by your virtuous works.*

All good deeds are luminous, but bad deeds are full of darkness. The fire ceremony is far superior to those ceremonies that are performed for totally selfish purposes. The selfish actions and rituals performed by the ignorant lead them to further darkness.

In this verse, "the luminous oblations" means that at the moment of virtuous thought, feeling, and deed, the performer's thoughts, speech, and deeds remain at peace and are full of joy. When one remains in inner tranquility and joy, one gains the inspiration to attain the higher rungs of the ladder of spirituality.

Jivatman, the individual soul, is like the sun in human life. Such an aspirant is guided directly by the deva, the inner dweller who witnesses all thoughts, feelings, and actions of the human being.

Good deeds lead one to heavenly joys, and the highest heaven or realm is called brahmaloka—the heaven of Brahma—which lasts for a longer time than the heaven ordinarily described or inferred by scriptures and aspirants respectively.

Good deeds, therefore, can only lead the aspirant to the heaven of Brahma, the highest of heavens, but have no power to bestow the grace of emancipation. Heaven is not at all related to the union of the individual soul— jivatman—with the cosmic soul, Brahman.

The greatest of rewards that can be attained through the worship performed by people who are devoid of knowledge is described here. Actually, such worship is the result of avidya or lack of real knowledge. Lack of real knowledge leads the aspirant to the world of material gain and happiness. It does not have the capacity to liberate the aspirant from the rounds of birth, growth, death, and decay.

Desire and longing for material happiness bring the aspirant back to the world again. Therefore, comparatively, even such good acts are inferior to the path of pure light and happiness brought about by the spiritual knowledge of Brahman.

VERSE 7:

> *Composed of eighteen constituents (the five elements,*
> *the ten senses, mind, ego, and intellect), this raft of life,*
> *which serves as a ground for performing the sacrifices,*
> *is not itself anchored securely, and thus remains adrift.*

The human body is like a raft; the two pranas are the oars, and the mind is the anchor. If all are healthy, the boat of life can be used to sail to the other shore of the ocean of samsara. The eighteen performers of agnihotra are compared to eighteen priests. The yajna is to be performed in the city of life by the individual soul and its wedded wife, higher buddhi.

All the eighteen components and members have been described in this verse. They are incapable of performing a ceremony which can lead the aspirant to his final goal of life, the attainment of Absolute Truth or Brahman.

As we have already said, the eighteen members (sixteen priests, the performer, and his wife) are important while performing the ceremony. Yet this ceremony is inferior, because it is performed without having the knowledge of Brahman, meditation, and contemplation. In fact, the group members performing the ceremony are liable to destroy the ceremony because they are performing the ceremony for external joy and without spiritual wisdom.

Just as the wine in a chalice is destroyed if the chalice is destroyed, so that neither the chalice nor the wine can be used in performing the mass, similarly, that which is subject to change, death, and decay cannot contain that which is imperishable.

Due to the absence of knowledge, a human being remains in darkness. Although a human being is a finite vessel, he carries infinity, no matter where he moves. But because of his own ignorance in identifying himself with the finite, he suffers.

Shankara, the great philosopher, says that cause and effect are inseparable. The effect is determined by the cause. The Imperishable cannot be attained by a perishable cause. As is true of the fire ceremony, so also is it true of the worship and deeds performed in the world—they are performed through perishable instruments; they are not everlasting. That which is not everlasting cannot produce immortality, emancipation, and the highest good.

In this verse, avidya—ignorance—and the deeds performed in ignorance, both externally and internally, are condemned, so that the aspirant learns to go beyond the mire of delusion created by the senses, sense objects, mind, and the desire to enjoy the pleasures of the world.

VERSE 8:

> *Fools are caught in the snare of ignorance, yet*
> *consider themselves to be wise. Caught in the*
> *unending cycle of pain and misery, they lead their*
> *lives as the blind are led by the blind.*

The eighth verse makes the aspirant aware of the deeper aspect of sadhana (spiritual practice), by saying that fools suffer on account of their own ignorance and thoughts, feelings, and desires. However, those who are considered to be wise and learned and yet are puffed up with pride and conceit only feed their own vanity. Such scholarship is equally condemnable; scholars may teach and preach the religious scriptures to others, but themselves remain in darkness. They wander about afflicted by many ills in life. They are like the blind leading the blind, for their teachings do not help eliminate ignorance. As long as one remains blindfolded and does not make a sincere effort, he cannot become a seer. Without becoming a seer, one cannot see the things of the world as they are and remain unattached. Deep in the heart of this multiplicity of forms, there dwells one Absolute Truth. An ignorant and blind person cannot guide the masses and, if he does, the "blind will lead the blind."

This verse silently suggests that a blind teacher is unable to help his students on the path of light. Blind are those who have created a strong barrier of ego, which does not allow them to go beyond. Without surrendering the ego, they remain vain. The Book of Ecclesiastes says, "Vanity of vanities; all is vanity." For such, darkness, darkness, everything is darkness.

This verse is also related to the previous verse, which explains that an aspirant should not be deluded into thinking that actions performed by him—whether they are ritualistic or deeds performed in daily life—will be helpful on the path of enlightenment. Without knowledge, liberation cannot be attained.

VERSE 9:

> *Like children, fools remain caught in the snare of*
> *ignorance, yet think that they have attained the*
> *highest goal of life. Due to attachment, they do not*

understand the essence of karma; therefore, after
exhausting the fruits of their virtuous deeds, they
fall back into the cycle of birth and death.

In this verse, it is said that the performers of rituals or karma are exactly like children who delight in ignorance. Playing with their toys and living in a limited world of immature
thinking, they constantly flatter themselves with the notion
that they have already accomplished the purpose of life. This is
because they do not know the Truth and they remain blinded
by their attachments. They build a house in the sand, which
falls down in the first shower of rain, like a house of cards falls
with the touch of a finger. Children and ignorant people are
alike because they are not aware of the transitory nature of
the objects of the world, and instead take delight in building
houses of sand.

Even if such individuals go to heaven, they fall back to earth
and suffer the miserable consequences of their desire to enjoy
the objects of the senses. The Upanishad explains that ritualistic worship performed without knowledge can never lead to
enlightenment. It also explains that heavenly joys are experienced by those who perform good deeds, good actions, and
rituals rightly.

We come to the conclusion that the joy experienced in heav-
en is not everlasting; therefore, it is impermanent. This momentary happiness can never be the ultimate goal of human life.
Therefore, aspirants should not waste their lifespan, which is
invaluable in the pursuit of Truth, in merely performing actions
selfishly for sensory gratification.

The aspirant on the path of sadhana is again and again
warned by the mantras of this Upanishad that the charms,

temptations, and attractions of the external world have their limitations. They are like weeds floating on the surface of the lake of life and cannot satisfy the aspirant's inner thirst. Though chewing such a weed will give momentary satisfaction, it will never be able to really quench one's thirst.

How can a human being presume that there can be a higher joy or highest good? There are two *anandas* a human being can experience. One kind of joy, such as sexual joy, is experienced by ordinary human beings. Such joys last for some time and then one again wants to indulge in them. Beneath these enjoyments, there is one desire that always lurks and prompts the aspirant to attain the highest of joys, which is everlasting—the joy of unity with the Absolute.

A simple analysis here will help one decide that worldly joys are short-lived and are experienced for a brief time, while the joy of the unity of the individual soul with Brahman is everlasting and never-changing. That is why it is said: "not *vishayananda* but *paramananda*—not sensual joys, but the joy of the everlasting."

In this verse, the phrase "foolish like children" means those who are not mature enough to be aware of the goal of life. This is one category of fools; but there is another category of fools that is composed of those who are more engrossed in the ways of the ignorant because of their attachments and pleasure-seeking philosophy. Still, an ignorant person is an ignorant person.

This verse states that without eliminating attachments and passions, spiritual knowledge does not arise. The joys of the sensory gratifications that one delights in are short-lived, and when the fruits of these actions are exhausted, one again falls back into the cruel clutches of avidya or ignorance.

VERSE 10:

> *Considering religious activities and mere public*
> *charity projects to be supreme, ignorant people do*
> *not recognize the highest good. Having enjoyed*
> *the fruits of their virtuous deeds in heaven, they*
> *return to the lower planes of existence.*

This verse starts with the phrase *ishta purta*. *Ishta* denotes all the possible deeds (including the fire ceremony) that a householder performs in the world, even the learning of the Vedas. *Purta* means doing charitable deeds selflessly for the good of others and serving others who need your help.

These meritorious actions, when performed with selfish motives, lead one to heavenly joys, but all the joys of earth and heaven are transitory. Those who are not mature and have not analyzed the difference between temporary joy and permanent happiness think that these charitable deeds will liberate them from their ignorance.

A fool is deluded by ignorance and becomes attached to family members, friends, and the objects of the world. Those who have made their life's goal that of obtaining worldly goods are not aware of the ultimate Truth, which has the power to bestow upon them the shower of imperishable joy. The means to final blessedness is the knowledge of the Self—the Self of all.

It is a law of the physical world that a human being cannot live without performing actions. We can divide human actions into three categories—good, bad, and mixed. If a good action is performed, one reaps the fruits of his deeds and is comfortable in modern life. If bad actions prevail, one remains depressed and negative and suffers the pangs of misery created by his own desires and actions. Those who perform mixed actions have the opportunity to become aware of the spiritual dimensions in life one day.

The scriptures say that bad actions lead to an animal life, good actions lead to spirituality, and mixed actions lead to rebirth in a human body. Acts of worship performed under the influence of ignorance are inadequate, and philanthropic work done with selfish motivation is also inferior to the knowledge of spirituality.

Those who perform charitable or philanthropic works to satisfy their hidden lust for "name and fame" develop a guilty conscience, which haunts their internal being, even though they may have a smile on their face from the praise, publicity, and honor given to them by others.

Performing such deeds, even if they are of the highest degree, will not eliminate the serious internal chasm of sorrow created by this division: inside, the person is one way but he or she acts differently in the external world. This serious division created by conflicting thoughts and deeds will never comfort a human being. Such philanthropic deeds, which only satisfy the human ego, are not healthy and not worthy of being taken as an example.

Of course, if philanthropic work is done as a way of purifying ego problems, then it expands the awareness of the human being. But there is still no karma that has the power to lead one to final liberation. Karma and knowledge are two opposite ends of the line of human life, and between these two ends extends the line called *life*. Knowledge alone liberates.

Truly selfless service is rendered only by those who are enlightened, have completed their share of worldly duties, and who are on the path of light because they have decided that karma is not the way. The way of liberation is knowledge. After a potter has made his pots, the wheel continues to rotate. Such a rotating wheel still has momentum, but the potter is free from the fruits of the wheel's rotation. Similarly, actions performed by the great sages do not affect their spiritual practice, and these deeds become a means on the path of spirituality.

VERSE 11:

> *Living in solitude, content with the food they*
> *receive as alms, observing the discipline of tapas*
> *and having firm faith, the wise with serene and*
> *purified minds enter through the gate of the*
> *sun the realm wherein dwells that immortal,*
> *unchanging, eternal* **purusha,** *the supreme Self.*

Most fortunate are those who enjoy the solitude of forest dwellings, leading a spiritual life and following spiritual disciplines with mind, action, and speech. They are peaceful. They spend their time in meditation, follow the system of meditation accurately, and ultimately go through the solar gate, where his majesty, the Immortal Being resides.

Such great men and women, free from impurities, remove all the obstacles and tread the path of light, leaving their footprints for other aspirants to follow. That is why it is said: "*Mahajano yena gattah sa pantha*—Follow the path of the great, ancient sages, for they have left their footprints for others to follow." Having completed the householder's duty, the wise utilize the remainder of their time and energy in the forest dwellings. They are called vanaprastha. This is the third rung on the ladder of attainment, or the third stage of life according to the ancients. When selfish deeds are abandoned and selfless deeds are performed, and when the senses do not disturb the tranquil mind, then inner serenity is experienced.

There are formulas and regulations prescribed by the Vedas and Upanishads for the third and fourth stages of life. These aspirants have adequate time and opportunity to meditate and create the fire of knowledge so that they can burn all their good and bad samskaras. The path they tread is called *devayana*—the path of light. That is the highest of all heavens in the relative universe. Such a person is called immortal because he attains the plane of immortal Brahma, yet his immortality lasts for one complete cycle only.

These verses describe the systematic and gradual step-by-step path of attaining liberation, which is called *karma mukti*. Such accomplished sages dwell in brahma-loka, absorbed in contemplation, and then attain final liberation after the end of the cycle.

According to the Advaita school of non-duality, the final liberation is attained through the pure knowledge of the attributeless Brahman, which can be realized here and now, in this lifetime. Those aspirants who pursue the knowledge of attributeless Brahman but drop their bodies before attaining the Absolute also attain the highest of heavens.

VERSE 12:

> *After examining the objects of the world that one*
> *has gained through one's karma, the knower of*
> *Brahman reaches a state of dispassion and non-*
> *attachment and realizes that the highest cannot*
> *be attained through mere actions. In order to*
> *know that, the aspirant should present himself,*
> *with all his humility, to a guru who is learned and*
> *established in Brahman consciousness.*

This verse actually guides the sincere aspirant and reveals a preliminary path to tread before he or she attains the knowledge of the scriptures and learns to meditate. One who is inclined to spiritual knowledge is a brahmana. Such an aspirant is free from the passions of the world. Having no worldly desires or attachments, he takes fuel in his hands and approaches a preceptor who is well-versed in the scriptural knowledge and, at the same time, is established in the consciousness of Brahman.

The student should not search for a preceptor under the pressure of emotionality or insecurity, but should be prepared by analyzing the nature of the external world, its objects, and the deeds performed. Good deeds performed by a human being bring good results. The performance of selfless deeds becomes a means toward spirituality and inspires one to attain the final liberation.

With firm determination and one-pointed desire, the aspirant goes to the preceptor "with fuel in hand," which denotes that the remaining subtle samskaras will be burned with the help and teachings of the preceptor, who has already realized the One. Fortunate are those who meet such a preceptor. Meeting such a preceptor is like being reborn.

Actually, according to the scriptures, there are three devas. The first is the mother who teaches, nourishes, dresses, and gives the child her complete, loving care and helps him to grow. She is called *matri deva*. The Sanskrit word *matri* means "mother" in English.

The second is the father who guides the growth of the child and gives all his support and affection. The father makes the child understand the world around him and teaches him to stand on his own feet.

When one becomes an adult and scrutinizes all the phases of life, from childhood onward, he examines the limits of worldly joys and understands the pairs of opposites—pain and pleasure—equally. As a householder, he then becomes frustrated, because the sensual joys in the world are only momentary and create attachments that are injurious and lead to barriers in his growth.

This analysis leads him to retire, but this retirement is actually a retirement from attachment. He has grown by leading a householder's life. He realizes that his goal is to attain Absolute Truth. Such an aspirant seeks a preceptor called *guru deva,* one who imparts spiritual knowledge and is totally selfless and full of love and compassion. This verse describes the right way of approaching the preceptor.

There is an important saying that when a disciple is ready, the guru appears. Searching for a guru is in vain, but preparation is important. Finally, "similar meets similar"; this is a universal law.

Fortunate is he who becomes aware of the necessity of treading the path of enlightenment and who finds a totally selfless master. A guru or master can give the aspirant that which cannot be given by anyone else. It is by God's grace that one meets such a guru.

In the modern world, there is so much exploitation that there are more gurus than disciples. The gurus search for disciples, instead of disciples searching for the guru. This epoch is *kali yuga* (age of darkness), and in kali yuga, as a previous verse says, "the blind lead the blind." They both remain in perdition, and neither can be emancipated.

VERSE 13:

> *That learned teacher imparts the essence of*
> *brahma vidya, the knowledge of Brahman, to the*

student who has approached him with reverence,
whose mind is calm and tranquil, and who has
achieved self-discipline. Such a student recognizes
the eternal purusha, pure consciousness and truth.

When the seeker's mind is purified by spiritual practices given by the guru, and when the mind establishes itself in the state of tranquility and equilibrium, then the sovereign science—the science of Brahman, the very basis of all sciences—is imparted by the preceptor or guru.

Those who are seeking with sincerity and who are determined to tread the path of spirituality first need to complete certain preliminary or preparatory steps. The initial step is to develop a tranquil mind, which is not possible without having learned how to consciously withdraw the senses from the charms and temptations of the world.

Here, the verse imparts knowledge to the teacher also, reminding that a wise teacher does not impart the knowledge of Brahman to impure, unprepared, or uncontrolled aspirants. The wise teacher should accurately impart the methods of the sovereign science through which the immutable and true purusha is attained. A wise guru gives instructions both in theory and practice.

The use of the word *purusha* indicates that one should first learn to practice the inward method of meditation, which makes him aware of the atman sleeping in the inner chamber of his being. Purusha means "one who sleeps in the city of life." This clearly means that the aspirant learns the path of meditation and contemplation.

Some modern teachers today think that by teaching the scriptures they will help students to attain Absolute Truth. This is not true: without the systematic methods of meditation, contemplation, and prayer combined, one cannot dig deep to uncover the immortal jewel of atman, which sleeps in the city of life.

This luminous Self is obscured from human view because it remains hidden behind the senses, breath, and mind—both conscious and unconscious. The method that leads the student beyond these is imparted by the teacher.

Etymologically, purusha means "that which fills all, that which dwells in the body *(puranatvat).*" All aspirants need a personal God, and that is their inner- dwelling Self. Finally, they realize that atman is Brahman. The word *purusha* is also used to refer to a person. Actually, we are all purushas, provided we are aware of the force sleeping within us and make a sincere attempt to know that center of consciousness that liberates us from all bonds.

The purusha within us is the very existence and support of our lives on the earth, without which all the components of the body cannot function. When the individual soul or purusha drops the garment called the body, the body becomes dust. Many ignorant people adore the body and are not aware of the purusha within. They look after the body but they are not aware of why they look after the body, thinking they exist to eat, drink, and sleep. When one becomes aware of the true Self within, then such an aspirant uses the mind, senses, breath, and body as instruments and becomes constantly aware of atman. Such a knower remains free from all pain and misery and wanders on this platform freely and fearlessly.

Here ends the second canto of Chapter 1.

Chapter
2

Mundaka
Upanishad

CANTO 1

VERSE 1:

It is the truth that, just as a great fire manifests thousands of sparks that share its nature, so the manifold world evolves from the Indestructible and is absorbed back into It again.

This verse starts with the statement: "This is the truth. Just as sparks rise from the blazing fire, similarly the universe issues forth, O my friend." Many beings and creatures having different names and forms have risen from the one Absolute Imperishable and verily, they all go back to their origin.

Absolute Truth refers to: 1) that which is self-existent; that which was never born, and therefore never dies, 2) that which is imperishable and everlasting, and 3) that which alone has the power to liberate one. It is true that the goal of human life is to attain the Absolute Truth, but aspirants find a great wall standing in front of them. As long as human beings are not aware of the center of consciousness within, their mind and senses lead them to the external world, which is full of distortions and dissipations.

When aspirants learn to train their mind, they become aware of Truth and live in the world like the lotus flower that grows in a pool, but whose petals remain above the water and unaffected by it. The technique of living in the external world should be practiced—not with attachment, but with love. Love and attachment are two opposing principles. Attachment contracts the human personality, while love expands it.

Many people think that they cannot survive without attachments. This is true; they survive temporarily only to finally destroy themselves with the black force of attachment. Attachment is like the veiler of the night who always delights in doing things in darkness, never in light. But those who understand the difference between attachment and love know that *attachment* means lust while *love* means selfless giving. Love is a great power that has liberating qualities. Love for God and attachment to lust are two entirely different motivations and have vastly different consequences. When one learns to live in the world doing his duties lovingly and skillfully, then he or she remains unattached, unaffected, and liberated from the bondage of karma and the fruits of action that one receives due to karma. Such human beings are aware that although attachment is the cause of all misery, love is the very nature of life, and is a liberating force that comforts them in all conditions and circumstances of life.

When the aspirant has firm faith in the Lord of life, atman, his own indweller, then he knows his individual Self, his eternal spark arising from its immortal source, Brahman.

Physics teaches that all life is like a particle or a wave. The Upanishads also say that this is true, that life is a wave of bliss in the vast ocean of bliss. Each wave rises from, and again subsides into, the same ocean. From the standpoint of Advaita, there is no death or birth. The life force is never born, nor does it die. When the aspirant firmly believes in the existence of the individual soul, not as a part and parcel of the Absolute Truth, but identical to, and essentially one with it, then he or she wants to directly experience that immeasurable, imperishable joy.

VERSE 2:

> *Purusha, the supreme Consciousness, is self-effulgent, formless, and unborn. It pervades and permeates the entire external and internal world. It is beyond prana and mind; it is perfect and unalloyed.*

When the aspirant, with the help of contemplation and meditation, crosses the mire of delusion created by his own ignorance, and when he directly experiences that his individual soul is the Self of all, then he knows that the Self is resplendent and without any form. There is no origin to it, but it is self-existent, pure purusha. The Self does not need prana or mind to support its self-existent reality.

The aspirant knows Him within himself and then finds Him as well in the external world. He transcends all that is relative. This is the self-luminous Reality. There is no birth, there is no death, and there are no modifications; therefore, there is no death or decomposition.

The knower of Brahman realizes the Absolute Truth to be without prana, mind, senses, or body. No attributes can be imposed on the pure Brahman, but in association with maya, which is Brahman's own power, it is the cause of manifestation. Whenever the Upanishadic mantra describes Brahman as a cause of manifestation, it refers to the saguna Brahman—Brahman with attributes.

The student who successfully treads the path of light with the help of self-analysis and self-control finally realizes the finer aspects of life and then attains the highest good—self-realization.

VERSE 3:

From this evolves prana (life energy), the mind,
all the senses, space, air, fire, water, and the earth,
which supports the whole world.

This verse describes how the human being has come into existence and, at the same time, how the aspirant understands that birth and death are illusory. Actually, the manifestation of the different names and forms of the universe do not have an existence of their own, but they exist because Absolute Truth exists. It is through nescience, or maya, that the pure and splendid, self-luminous Brahman appears as the universe and its numerous objects.

Both before and after the manifestation of the universe, Brahman is free from prana, mind, sense organs, and forms and names. They are the forms of saguna Brahman. According to the Upanishadic philosophy, these projections and modifications are therefore unreal. Just as various ornaments made out of the same gold have no existence independent of the gold, so similarly, do the various objects and forms have no existence of their own. They are mere words used for convenience and communication in day-to-day life, rather than real entities, just as a childless woman cannot be called a mother simply because she dreams about having a son.

The manifestation of this universe is like a dream. Just as a dream is real to the dreamer, so is the universe real to the ignorant or un-illumined one. Such ignorant persons continue to live in the darkness of ignorance until they are awakened to the light of Absolute Truth.

VERSE 4:

> *Fire is the head; the moon and sun are eyes. The*
> *directions are the ears. The revealed Vedas are His*
> *speech. Air is His prana. This universe is His heart.*
> *Earth itself has emerged from His feet, and He*
> *alone is the inner self of all living beings.*

In this verse, the first embodied manifestation of the Lord has the totality of the names and forms of the universe. It describes Brahman, but this description is actually that of saguna Brahman—Brahman with attributes. Brahman without attributes cannot be described.

The verse says that certainly He is the indwelling atman within all. The word "fire" can be interpreted in many ways in the Vedic literature. As we have already said, it has more than three hundred meanings. Literally, "agni" means fire, although at times it is used to mean heaven, too.

In describing saguna Brahman, the verse says that fire is his head, the sun and moon are his eyes, and the four directions or quarters are his ears. The knowledge of the Vedas, which has been revealed to the rishis, is his voice, the wind is his breath, and the whole universe is his heart. This earth of ours has originated from his feet.

This verse describing saguna Brahman or *virat purusha*— the first embodied manifestation, which is also the same as the inner Self of all beings—is said to be infinite and all-pervading.

The previous verse refers to the purusha as the individual soul, sleeping in the city of life within the human body. This verse guides the aspirant to understand that the individual self, purusha, is the same as the universal self called *virat.* One dwells in the human body, the other dwells in the universe. The *Ishopanishad* says that the Absolute Brahman dwells in the smallest of the particles and is, at the same time, all-pervading in the universe.

The aspirant then understands that the superimposition of the body, breath, senses, and mind is not real but illusory, and the Self is the Supreme Self. This state of self-realization liberates him from the self-created barriers and the obstacles of his petty-mindedness.

The tangible universe is a modification of the mind. It is not perceived in deep sleep because in deep sleep, it disappears. The mind is capable of producing numerous tangible forms. All the forms and names are created by the cosmic mind. As all individuals have their own minds, so is the cosmic individual the totality of all minds. The cosmic mind is shakti, through which virat can be understood. If an aspirant learns to train his mind, he will be able to fully understand his senses, body, and all the internal elements therein. However, as an instrument, the mind itself is not capable of leading the aspirant on the path of self-realization.

When the mind does not continue to create barriers and obstacles, this quality of mind is called "sattvic mind." When the mind is sattvic it becomes easy for the aspirant to go beyond the usual mire of delusion created by the mind itself: "I am small, I have a small form, I am this form." This type of thinking is a creation of the mind. As long as aspirants identify themselves with the thoughts, feelings, and objects of the mind, they can never establish themselves in their essential nature, which is atman. But the mind that is disciplined, trained, and purified does not stand as a wall. The aspirant then fathoms the boundaries and fields of the mind, both conscious and unconscious.

VERSE 5:

> *Having the sun as its source of energy, fire evolves*
> *from Him. From Him also evolves soma (the*
> *second stage of fire). From soma comes rain, and*
> *from that, all the herbs that grow on the earth. Just*
> *as a man plants a seed in a woman and thus life*
> *ensues, so with the aid of purusha, do numberless*
> *beings evolve.*

This verse also describes and expands upon the attributes of virat purusha, explaining that heaven is the first projection of virat purusha, and the sun is its fuel. The moon in the heaven bestows its shower of blessings on the earth—the rain and rain clouds—which are classified as the second fire. The herbs grow from the earth, which is the third fire. The herbs are eaten by men and that is the fourth fire. Then, man casts forth seed and sows it in woman, which is the fifth fire. In this manner, many creatures are born from the virat purusha—the all-pervading Being.

This verse refers to the five fires described in *Chhandogya Upanishad*. According to that story, Shvetaketu, who was a son of the rishi named Gautama, visited a great king of Panchala. The king asked the boy if he knew how the offerings made at the sacrifices were transformed into human bodies. Neither the boy nor his father could answer the question, so the king explained the matter by describing the five fires indicated above.

The reader should not be confused because of the word *agni* or *fire*. Verily, this is all fire. Life is sustained by fire: breath is fire, prana is fire. The mind functions because of fire. Therefore, when we talk of fire sadhana, it refers to the fire of knowledge as well.

There are many subtle symbols in the Upanishads. Without knowing those symbols in their profundity, the teachings will remain obscure. A competent teacher teaches both the theory and practice of the scriptures. The theory gives the knowledge of the profound philosophy of the universe and its creation. The practice of contemplation and meditation helps one to realize that the individual self is the same Self of all.

VERSE 6:

> *From Him also come forward the mantras of the* Rig, Sama, *and* Yajur Vedas, *the knowledge pertaining to initiation, rituals, the sacrifices, and the concept of giving offerings. From Him also develop the units of time (such as the year and the month), and the aspirants who strive to perform rituals, as well as the whole world, which is purified, illuminated, and sustained by soma and surya (fire and the source of fire).*

This verse again repeats that from Him comes the knowledge of the *Rig, Sama,* and *Yajur Vedas,* as well as the *Atharva Veda.* Sacred chants and all the rules and regulations of the ceremonies originate from the same source—virat purusha. The *Rig Veda* contains Vedic mantras in verse as well as the rules and regulations and metric systems *(chhandas)* for mantras, as in the *Gayatri mantra.*

The *Sama Veda* consists of the mantras and their various classifications. These mantras are set to music, from which the classical music of India originates. All keynotes are described in the *Sama Veda.* The *Yajur Veda* mainly consists of mantras in prose form. These scriptures prescribe numerous methods for conducting ceremonies, which have their origin in spirituality. During that period, the ancients performed many ceremonies to strengthen the awareness of Brahman.

VERSE 7:

> *From Him evolve manifold celestial beings,*
> *evolved souls with full awareness of their goal*
> *(sadhyas), human beings, animals, birds, prana*
> *and apana, all kinds of grains, tapas, faith, truth,*
> *discipline of mind and senses, and many other*
> *rules and laws.*

From Him—the virat purusha, the universal being—arise the finer forces of life, celestial beings called "bright beings" or devas, men, beasts and birds, prana and apana, inhalation and exhalation, grains, austerity, faith, truth, continence, and the law.

This verse creates an affirmative attitude in the mind of the aspirant—that all the objects of the world and their forms have originated from Brahman. Brahman is the only cause. Such an attitude, if cultivated, gives faith and inner serenity to the aspirant, which helps him to tread the path of light.

All the actions performed by both ignorant and wise men are regarded as sacrificial acts. The ceremonies and all their ancillaries, including the results, have their origins in Brahman.

VERSE 8:

> *From Him evolve the sevenfold pranas, the seven*
> *flames, the seven fuels, the seven kinds of offerings,*
> *and the sevenfold universe. Residing in the cave of*

**the body, the heart, the sevenfold pranas continue
their journey.**

From Brahman alone proceed the seven pranas, which
remain in the reservoir in the human head—the two eyes, the
two ears, two nostrils, and mouth. They are also taken to mean
the seven rishis. The seven acts of sensation created by the sev-
en pranas are called the seven flames. The pranas are ablaze and
are lit by objects.

The seven kinds of knowledge are actually seven sensations,
which are called oblations. There are seven flames in the human
body, which are the seven chakras, where the pranas dwell on
every plane. Here, the word *prana* is not used as a vital force,
but that which functions in the two eyes, two ears, two nostrils,
and mouth. However, because of their different functions, all
the pranas operate in each center in a spiritual way, which is
coordinated by the mind.

These different pranic vehicles function all the time, even
during deep sleep, and their functioning is experienced by the
yogis in the heart. In this verse, the word *cave* has been used
for both the body and the heart. The body is a cave in which
dwells the inner being, and the heart is a cave in which dwells
the Innermost Being. But inside the body, the heart is the main
center from where the functioning of the body is controlled. It
is this *heart* that controls the physical heart and brain, too.

Yoga science describes more than 72,000 channels of
pranic energy and their vehicles. Prana in this instance refers
to the vital force, the first unit of life, but that first unit of life
is also inseparably related to the universal life with the help of
the vehicle that supplies prana constantly. There are ten major
pranic vehicles; but in this Upanishad, only seven pranas are

described in order to intrigue students, so that they will explore the functioning of the pranic vehicles in the human body.

When aspirants learn the internal fire ceremony, then they use the objects of the senses as offerings for the sacrificial fire.

VERSE 9:

From this supreme Being spring the various
oceans, mountains, and rivers, and all the herbs.
Within all this resides the inner Self.

From Him arise all oceans, rivers, and mountains, and from Him alone come forth all plants, flowers, their flavors, and fragrances. From Him also come herbs and grains, which are consumed and through which the subtle body is encircled by the gross elements of matter. From Him come foods derived from plants, herbs, and the other sources of the earth, which sustain the physical body. Nowhere does this Upanishad mention that animals are sacrificed in any of the ceremonies or that they are meant to be eaten by human beings. The foods that are derived from plants and herbs—such as rice, barley, wheat, and vegetables—are healthy foods for maintaining the physical body.

Meat eaters are also called "secondary vegetarians," because they eat the meat of animals who eat vegetables. Research has shown that a vegetarian diet is very healthy and helpful on the path of spirituality. Such a diet is available everywhere and anywhere, in every corner of the earth. If one acquires a simple knowledge of nutrients—minerals, vitamins, proteins, and carbohydrates—he or she will see that a vegetarian diet leads the aspirant to good health, both physically and mentally. On the path of spirituality, vegetarian food suits the aspirant. This is not to say that a non-vegetarian cannot tread the path of spirituality, but an aspirant should learn to lead a simple life, and most of the great sages and scholars of the ancient times lived on a vegetarian diet and lived long and healthy lives.

In order to live a long and healthy life, there are also other considerations besides simply eating nutritious foods. These include a knowledge of the science of breath and breathing exercises, which are important in helping one to attain a healthy life. We consider health on all dimensions—physical, mental, and spiritual. Cheerfulness is the greatest of physicians; a positive attitude toward life is necessary to maintain health. Even if one eats a nutritious diet, if one is experiencing the pressure of mental agony or emotional pain, this can sometimes convert food into "poisons." Therefore, a state of mental cheerfulness is equally as important as the food itself in helping one to live a healthy life.

It is also traditionally said that excessive roasting and toasting of food turns organic calcium into inorganic calcium, for which there is no use in the human body. This puts undue pressure on the kidneys and disturbs the metabolism. Simple nutritious foods, properly baked and cooked and then eaten in a cheerful and pleasant atmosphere seem to be most beneficial.

VERSE 10:

> *This whole universe is the expansion of purusha*
> *alone. Tapas, knowledge, and its result manifest*
> *from Brahman, and ultimately Consciousness*
> *is the essence of all that exists. He who knows*
> *purusha residing in the cave of the heart destroys*
> *the knot of ignorance here, in this lifetime.*

This verse states that everything is born of Brahman. He alone is the cause of all animate and inanimate objects of the world. For the aspirant, it is important to note that the supreme and immortal atman is hidden in the inner chamber of his or her heart, and by knowing it, all the knots of ignorance are cut asunder.

The purusha, the cosmic Self alone, is truly the universe. All the actions, austerities, penance, and manifestations have originated from that supreme Being, who remains sleeping in the cave of the heart. Again and again the Upanishadic teachings lead the aspirant to strengthen his faith and to realize that the universe is born from Brahman; it has no existence of its own. All actions and ceremonies have originated in Brahman. This Upanishad starts with the mantra pertaining to the question, "By knowing what, can all be known?" and the answer is given here: the universe and all animate and inanimate objects have arisen from Brahman, the supreme Self. Therefore, nothing can come out of Brahman but Brahman. By knowing Brahman, one knows the universe. An aspirant should attain this knowledge in this lifetime, on this earth. He or she attains this by dwelling in the body and identifying not with the objects of the world, but with atman. Such an attainment will lead the aspirant to the height of liberation, which is jivanmukti—liberation in this body in this lifetime.

Here ends the first canto of Chapter 2.

CANTO 2

VERSE 1:

Here (in this body) is contained a Great Light.
Known by the name guhachara, *the cave dweller,*
that great truth has been endowed right here. All
that which animates, flickers, feels, and has the
appearance of existence or nonexistence—all is
established in It. By attaining the knowledge of the
supreme Light, a seeker surpasses all living beings.

This verse describes the Almighty as the inner dweller in the innermost chamber of everyone's heart. That luminous Light of lights is known to move there. This is the most powerful support of all, just as the hub supports the spokes of a wheel. It is the cause of everything that moves, blinks, and breathes. "O disciple, know this luminous One as your own real Self." That which is both gross and subtle and beyond the senses and mind is unknown to all creatures. It is Brahman's energy that makes all senses, pranas, and the mind function. The senses of hearing, thinking, and seeing exist because of the power of Brahman, the inner dweller.

Without this very source of energy, the senses, breath, and mind are inert and have no power to function. It is Brahman that appears to be the individual soul. That is why the sensations of sight, sound, taste, smell, and touch are experienced. The aspirant should contemplate Brahman as the Self that is the source of all these experiences. The aspirant experiences Brahman as the very heart, and as the knower and seer. It is the presence of the Self that shines forth through all the states of mind. Therefore, the Self appears to be moving. It is exactly like the spokes of a wheel, which move because of the wheel's nave.

Those who are not disciplined do not understand the systematic way of contemplating the inner dweller. They can neither meditate nor focus their mind. Such a mind and intellect, which are undisciplined, have no power to know the inner Self. The Self is without form and therefore, it becomes difficult for the aspirant to focus his mind on the Self. Without form and name. Brahman is in the power of the atom and in the minutest particle we can imagine, and at the same time pervades the entire universe. Verse four of the *Ishopanishad* says: "The Self is one and unmoving, swifter than the mind."

Atman is identical to Brahman. When we describe the nature of the human being we emphasize that atman dwells in the cave of the human body. It is important for the aspirant to know that the nature of atman can be perceived by the eye of his or her inner mind. In this context it is said that atman is like the hub of a wheel, which causes the movement of the whole wheel, and yet does not itself move. *Ishopanishad* explains it in this manner: Mind is faster than light and yet atman is faster than the mind. This means that no matter how fast the mind runs, atman, being all-pervading, is already there.

VERSE 2:

> *This immutable Brahman is the light which is*
> *subtler than subtle. The whole world and all those*
> *who reside in the world are contained in this light.*
> *Brahman itself manifests into prana, speech, and*
> *mind. That alone is real. That is immortal, and it*
> *is This which should be known.*

The chariot moves because it is directed by an intelligent driver. Pure consciousness guides the pranas, mind, and senses, though it remains indivisible. The aspirants learn to contemplate the Truth, that Brahman dwells within the cave of the heart of every being. This gives them immense faith and, instead of looking at the external world, their minds spontaneously lead them to various inner dimensions of life and finally to self-realization. Contemplation and meditation should be thoroughly understood and practiced regularly without any break. Patanjali, the codifier of yoga science states: *"Sa tu dirgha-kala-nairantarya-satkarasevito dridha-bhumih*—That practice, however, becomes firm of ground only when pursued and maintained in assiduous and complete observance for a long time, without interruption, and with a positive and devout attitude."

To understand the sovereign science of Brahman, an aspirant should learn to sharpen the intellect and purify the mind and heart before he or she seeks to attain the kingdom of Brahman within. Brahman is the nucleus, and the universe is its expansion; atman is the nucleus in individual human life. The mind, intellect, senses, and pranas are His creations, which function according to His guidance.

Just as a scientist makes experiments in his laboratory, so does the aspirant make his internal life a laboratory for learning to understand the finest and subtlest power. Therefore, an aspirant should precisely follow the path of meditation and contemplation in a well-organized and systematic way, exactly as a scientist makes experiments in the lab.

Blind faith misleads the aspirant. Reasoned faith and a mind and intellect that are purified through spiritual discipline help the student to reach many unfathomable levels of life, which are not normally known by people with ordinary minds. And there is no other way of knowing except by the path of meditation and contemplation. In contemplation, the intellect is sharpened; in meditation, the mind, intellect, and other modifications unite and make a one-pointed effort with full *shraddha,* which means with devotion plus reverence.

Many students uselessly waste their time trying to argue that bhakti is higher than karma or that karma is higher than bhakti. Karma is definitely inferior to bhakti, but selfless karma, practiced as a worship, is a part of bhakti, and this path of bhakti or love leads one to realize the Self. Real aspirants practice meditation with full shraddha, and in their external life in the world do selfless actions instead of indulging in such futile discussions.

VERSE 3:

> *Holding the great bow of Upanishadic wisdom, the*
> *aspirant should fix the arrow of mind, sharpened*
> *with meditation, on its target. Draw the string*
> *with full absorption and shoot at the target. O my*
> *friend, remember immutable, eternal Truth alone*
> *is the target.*

The Upanishads praise the glory of the syllable *AUM* and prescribe meditating on the sound to lead the student to the fourth state. Practically all the Upanishads describe *AUM* as the highest syllable used in contemplation. Actually, one who knows this syllable in its profundity knows Brahman. The Upanishads prescribe a definite and positive method of meditation for renunciates or advanced students.

Without studying the scriptures such as the *Mandukya Upanishad,* beginners should not make an effort to use either the syllable *AUM* alone or its sound and meaning in order to focus their minds. *AUM* is a compound of three letters: A, U, and M, which represent the three states of consciousness normally experienced by jivatman—waking, dreaming, and sleeping. It also finally includes the fourth state, *turiya,* the superconscious state, which is silent and is pure atman.

Beginners, who are not well-versed in the scriptures, should learn to meditate and prepare themselves to understand the glory and meaning of the syllable *AUM.* Those who have crossed the limitations of the physical and mental and are mindful only of the spiritual path contemplate and meditate on *AUM.* They have left behind the use of concrete objects as focal points, such as those used by beginners, and have gone beyond the images and thought patterns created by the mind. They meditate on the sound *AUM.*

Seekers should understand that visualization leads seekers to visionary realms. Like great poets and artists who have a vision, the sage's knowledge does not come through the mind but through vision. The imagination of such great people is not the product of the mind itself, and therefore, the distractions and distortions of the mind have no power to tease or distort their pure imagination.

The aspirant should learn to sit in an erect posture, keeping the head, neck, and trunk straight. He or she gently closes the mouth and seals the teeth, so that the tongue does not move.

Then the aspirant learns to listen to the sound *AUM,* which does not create jerks or irregularities in the breath and which helps the pranic sheath to experience serenity.

There are very few mantras that can be classified as a foundation for the meditative method. Using other mantras in the breath can be fatal if they are not properly and accurately practiced by the aspirant.

One who knows both physical and yoga anatomy will understand that the constant creation of jerks in the breath makes the movement of the lungs and the pumping station of the heart irregular, which will then cause other irregularities in the supply of blood to the brain. Therefore, the process of imparting mantras is a great science, and only a few teachers and yogis understand the consequences of their use. We will explain this subject matter in greater detail later.

This verse says that when the aspirant has completed the preliminaries, such as the withdrawal of the senses, he or she then learns how to prepare the mighty bow made by the wisdom of the Upanishads. When the arrow of mind has been sharpened by meditation and fixed on the target with absorption, then the aspirant sends the arrow to its mark, the luminous Brahman.

VERSE 4:

> **AUM *is the bow, atman (individual self) is the arrow; Brahman (the universal self) is the target. Aim precisely and, like an arrow, become merged with the target.***

The fourth verse continues to explain that the mystic syllable *AUM* is used by advanced yogis and aspirants as the bow, and the Self, the jivatman, is used as an arrow. Such an aspirant makes Brahman the target. Only an undistracted, undissipated, and one-pointed mind will be capable of doing so. If the mind is not purified, made one-pointed and inward, then shooting arrows at the objects of the world will be of no benefit at all.

Constant japa, which is a great technique for making the mind one-pointed, is implied here. This syllable *AUM* is a mystical syllable too. It is mystical because it is beyond all names and forms. It is something abstract, relating to the different states and experiences of jivatman during the waking, dreaming, and sleeping states.

There is no mystery about this syllable and its sound to those who have studied the scriptures under the guidance of a well-versed preceptor and who have practiced the method of unifying contemplation *(vichara)* and meditation *(dhyana)* to make the mind one-pointed and inward.

If one constantly mentally remembers *AUM* without interruption by other thoughts, *AUM* will surely and properly create a deep groove in the unconscious mind. Eventually it will guide the student even during the time of transition, when the jiva leaves the body and no one else is capable of helping him.

AUM is considered to be a *setu,* or a bridge between the two shores. When the individual soul drops the body, there is a period of transition during which the jiva has to be all alone, travelling from this shore of life to the other shore. Utter darkness and loneliness are experienced by the jiva during this period, and there is no one to lead jiva at that time. Constant remembrance of the syllable *AUM,* and an understanding of its meaning with a feeling of devotion, will help the aspirant to continue to create a deep groove in the unconscious mind.

Then, at the time of death or departure—when the body, breath, and conscious mind fail, when there is complete isolation and separation from the external world, when there is no one to help—the great groove that was made by the aspirant's sincere efforts brings forward the merits stored in the reservoir of the unconscious. This helps one to create the bridge between this shore and the other shore of life, life hereafter.

Advanced and accomplished yogis practice a technique of death and dying and thus remain free from the fear of death because they have already built a bridge, although others are not able to do so. Those who are not advanced meditators are not capable of understanding, knowing, and practicing the technique of building the bridge. Therefore, they are deprived of knowing the most highly accomplished technique of yogic science. This verse is meant to create a particular awareness in the minds and hearts of advanced aspirants who are treading the luminous path of Brahman—self-realization.

VERSE 5:

> *Mind, the pranas, and the other elements,*
> *including heaven, earth, and all the spaces*
> *between, are held in Him. Know only that single*
> *atman; speak of nothing else. This knowledge is a*
> *bridge to immortality.*

When the aspirant's mind is purified by the methods of contemplation and meditation, he or she does not become distracted by worldly thoughts and their attachments. The preceptor who has established himself in Brahman consciousness *(shrautriya brahmanistha)* exhorts his student to renounce and give up all vain actions and to contemplate and meditate only on Brahman.

In Brahman alone are woven different levels of heaven, earth, the space between, the mind and its modifications, and the sense organs. The student realizes that pure atman—one without a second—is worth knowing and then no longer desires the transitory objects of the world.

A student is forcefully advised by his preceptor that the power of speech should be preserved and used in a proper manner. Giving up all other talk means that there is no talk except of Brahman. The student participates in *satsanga,* which means experiencing the company of the sages or conversing with the sages. This strengthens his awareness of Brahman. The dialogues between the student and preceptor pertain to Brahman. They never discuss anything about the mundane world.

For all aspirants, it is unhealthy to talk too much. Actually, talking too much is unhealthy in any walk of life. Those who talk too much usually speak nonsense. The aspirant on the path of spirituality is instructed to stop wasting his energy through foolish speech and is instructed to give up all vain actions, as described in the fourth verse. But the mind should not be allowed to remain without some pleasant talk. For the sincere aspirant, there cannot be anything pleasant except concentration on Brahman.

Atman is the inmost dweller of all living beings. Therefore, the focal point of concentration and meditation is only on atman, not on the other finer forces or the bright colors or lights flashing from the domain of atman.

Many times during meditation, when one element becomes predominant, its influence on the mind creates illusory visions for the aspirant in different lights, colors, and forms. These illusory experiences should be discarded. They do not mean anything; they are not spiritual experiences. All the experiences from the psychic world are inferior compared to the experience received from the spiritual level of life. Those who strive sincerely to attain atman automatically give up the interests that relate to both avidya (ignorance) and lower knowledge. Such experiences and knowledge are mixed and disturb the student. A hunch or intuition often rolls down from these realms of mind and gives a new experience to the aspirant. Such experiences coming from the lower knowledge, from the psychic fields and other levels of the interior life, should be ignored. They will prove to be harmful and distracting to aspirants.

Only the knowledge of the real Self will give the individual the strength to gain freedom from the mire of delusion created by avidya. By knowing the real Self, atman, one can gain freedom from the rounds of birth and death and go beyond these two deep habits. The habit of the body is death, and the habit of the mind for desire causes birth. To break these two habit patterns is possible only with the knowledge of luminous atman.

After making sincere efforts, the disciple receives blessings from his preceptor. "Blessings" and "grace" are two of the least understood of all words. People often use the word *blessing,* as in when they say, "My blessings are with you. May God bless you." But these are meaningless words unless one has done his duty faithfully and skillfully. Such an aspirant deserves to have blessings from the great sages who have the power to bless and bestow the shower of blessings upon their students. Then, the Lord Almighty blesses such aspirants.

There are two forces that are experienced on the journey to the Absolute. One is the ascending force, while the other is the descending force. The ascending force means the aspirant must make sincere efforts; the descending force means that grace flows freely to those who have accomplished their task truthfully and sincerely, with all their might through mind, action, and speech.

We actually receive grace from four sources. The first three are the grace of God, the grace of the guru, and the grace of the Bible or scriptures that you believe in. The fourth grace is the grace of the Self. This means that when one's own conscience approves one's actions, speech, thoughts, and especially spiritual practices, he or she then feels unbounded joy. That is the grace of the Self.

VERSE 6:

> *Just as the spokes of a chariot wheel come together in its hub, all the nadis (energy channels) in the human body meet in the heart, where He moves while manifesting in various ways. Meditate on* **AUM,** *which is one with the Self. May you reach the other shore beyond all darkness!*

This verse is very interesting and profound. After explaining the deeper meaning of the syllable *AUM* and the methods of contemplation and meditation, the scriptures say that atman becomes manifold within the cave of the heart. If you visit a Shiva temple, it is interesting to note that the temple is actually a symbolic representation of the heart. Within the four chambers, there is a *lingam* on which the nectar constantly drips, making the sound "lub dub," which is similar to the sound of a heartbeat.

In the human body, if this sound decreases or increases, it denotes that there is something wrong in the city of life. If the functioning of the heart is not properly regulated, death may result. The arteries and veins meet in the hub of the body, the heart; they do their respective jobs of nourishing and purifying the heart. Meditation on the inner hub, which is *AUM,* leads the student to an entirely new experience—crossing the mire of darkness.

Yogic science explains it in a precise manner. The anahata chakra (heart center) has its location between the upper and lower hemispheres of the body, each of which contains three chakras. Practices involving anahata chakra are always recommended to control *bhava,* which means to balance the emotional life as well as the problem of inertia or sleep. If a beginner is not yet competent to meditate on this chakra, he experiences sleep-like inertia or dozes.

In verse 6, the preceptor inspires the meditator because he is qualified for the attainment of knowledge that will help him to cross the sea of darkness.

VERSE 7:

> *He is omniscient and the source of all sciences. It is through His greatness that order is established on the earth. In the celestial realm of Brahman, in the eternal space of the heart, this atman alone resides. Manifesting in the form of mind, prana guides the functions of the body. While seated in the heart. He pervades the whole body. By attaining the knowledge of that blissful and immutable purusha, the knowers of Truth see all that shines.*

This verse describes the deeper significance of meditation on the anahata chakra. The inner dweller—atman, the knower of all—is a splendid glory in the world. He is all-wise and dwells in the space that is the abode of Brahman. It is the very source from which emanate all the forms in the mind, and it is this which makes the body and senses function.

His living presence is found inside the heart. That which shines as the immortal atman, the wise behold as the same Self of All. The anahata chakra is also called *brahmapuri*. This is not a reference to the physical heart; the physical heart itself is governed by the subtler power that dwells in the anahata chakra, situated in the center between the two breasts.

The preceptor instructs his disciples to meditate on the center of the luminous lotus, where the eternal jewel resides with all its beauty and grandeur. The light of that immortal jewel has no haziness, and a clouded mind is not able to visualize the light that permanently resides in the center of the lotus, in the inner chamber of the human being.

The Upanishads are expressed in a precise, poetic, and symbolic language. It becomes the duty of the teacher to first have the practical knowledge of the methods of meditation and then to teach the student the practical lessons imparted by these verses.

When the aspirant attains clarity of mind, then such a mind can clearly visualize the self-illumined Brahman residing in brahmapuri—the city of Brahman. The city of Brahman is like a fortress; it is the city of life. The five tattvas (earth, water, fire, air, and space) make a strong external, outermost wall of this city of life.

An inner wall is created by the senses. Still another wall further within is created by the thoughts, desires, and emotions. At the gate of this fortress of life, the two pranas—inhalation and exhalation—remain on guard, constantly defending the city of life. The innermost wall is constructed by the samskaras that hold the attachments and pleasure-seeking desires. When the mind is purified, clarity is attained. Such a mind is capable of receiving the vision of the self-luminous Brahman, in which there is no smoke, no darkness, and no death. This is the kingdom of immortality. This method of meditation is introduced by the competent teacher in gradual steps, and when the student realizes that law, beauty, power, and energy have been provided by Brahman, then he or she becomes enlightened.

VERSE 8:

Once both shores of life, here and hereafter, are known, the knot at the heart is destroyed, all doubts vanish, and the binding impact of all karma is destroyed.

For the aspirant who realizes the immutable Brahman in both the high and low, all the knots of ignorance are destroyed. All doubts vanish, and he is free from the bondage of karmas. This verse hints that self-realization is possible only in the human body. Therefore, when one possesses a human body, complete with breath, mind, and individual soul, one is called a person. Such a golden opportunity should not be wasted but utilized for self-realization. *Hridayagranthi* means the "knot of ignorance." When the knot of ignorance is destroyed, then all doubts automatically vanish.

Because of their clouded minds, ordinary human beings remain in doubt regarding the ultimate nature of things. But when doubt is dispelled, enlightenment dawns. The knot of ignorance and the knot of karma compose the nature of avidya, which has given pure atman the status of jivatman.

The student should understand three aspects of karma, or three effects of karma: *prarabdha, sanchita,* and *agamin.* Prarabdha refers to the results of the karmas that one has already performed. Such actions begin to germinate, bearing fruits in this lifetime. Sanchita refers to those which are stored for the future, while those coming to fruition in future lives are classified as agamin. This can be better understood with the help of an illustration.

An archer has a bow and arrow in his possession. The arrows he has already released are called prarabdha karma. The arrows which remain in his hand to be shot are called sanchita karma, and those arrows which remain in the quiver for the future are called agamin.

As a matter of fact, unless atman is realized by the aspirant, the law of karma creates a whirlpool for the human being. After realization, the present and future karmas and their binding effects are destroyed. But the past karmas and their fruits, until they are exhausted either through enjoyment or through suffering in the present life, do affect even realized ones. Unless the prarabdha, past karmas and their effects, are exhausted, total freedom is impossible.

Renunciates say, however, that even the effects of past karmas can be destroyed by lighting the fire of knowledge. It is still a matter of debate to some, but the law of karma seems to be inevitable. Of course, those who are realized attain a serene and unaffected state of being, like the lotus in the water.

VERSE 9:

> *In the innermost golden sheath resides pure and*
> *perfect Brahman. The knowers of atman realize*
> *this as the brightest of all bright lights.*

This verse says that self-illumined Brahman is the highest golden sheath. It is pure, the most brilliant of all brilliances. The yogic description is given briefly in this verse. There are five sheaths or *koshas* that cover the effulgent Brahman or atman.

These koshas are *annamaya, pranamaya, manomaya,* and the *vijnanamaya.* The fifth is *anandamaya*—the blissful sheath.

From behind the glittering curtain of anandamaya kosha peeks the great majesty full of brilliance—the indivisible Brahman, which is completely free from all taint of ignorance. Just as a sword is encased in a sheath, so does atman—the immortal jewel, the fountainhead of beauty, light, and life—reside in the golden bliss sheath. The wise know that He is the real Self, the Self of all.

Consider a lamp with five shades: the light that shines through these five coverings is very dim, but when we learn to take off all the sheaths, or find a way of penetrating all the sheaths, then we see the light clearly. The light of atman, full of brilliance, helps the buddhi to function. That is why buddhi is able to discriminate, decide, and judge. It also helps manas to function, and that is why manas can function both inside and outside the body. Because of their power, the two breaths constantly guard the city of life, and because of the support of atman, the five elements—earth, fire, water, air, and space—compose the body.

The wise perceive atman as the witness of the different states of mind. It is through the knowledge of the inner Self, through the knowledge of atman, that the aspirant attains emancipation. But emancipation cannot be attained by the study of subjects related to the external world or its objects.

VERSE 10:

> *In the realm of Brahman, neither the sun, stars, moon, nor lightning shine—not to speak of worldly fire. It is only when He shines that all these others may shine. It is through His light that this whole universe is illumined.*

As we have already indicated, there are innumerable galaxies, and every galaxy has a solar system. In our solar system, the sun that shines and illumines all the objects of the world, shines because of the power of Brahman. The shining power is not the sun's own inherent quality.

The innermost atman shines through all beings and smiles through all faces. Here, the sun that shines in our solar system is used as a symbol, for its light dispels the darkness of the earth, and yet the sun also becomes a symbol for aspirants to remain unaffected and above the world.

A student should learn to follow the example of the sun. The verse says that the light of the sun and the sun itself are merely symbols in the world. The sun borrows its shining light from its source, Brahman. This is also true in the case of the city of life; our buddhi, prana, and all the senses are illumined by the brilliance of atman.

Atman is verily Brahman and is real; It alone exists. All things endowed with name and form are nothing but the unchanging Absolute, self-existent Reality.

VERSE 11:

> *All this is immutable Brahman. Brahman is*
> *before, behind, to the right, to the left, above, and*
> *below all. This whole universe is an expansion of*
> *that highest Brahman.*

All the names and forms are projected by one Absolute Brahman, One without a second. The entire manifestation exists because of the existence of Brahman. The ignorant experience various names and forms, forgetting the existence of atman or Brahman. This delusion is created by the individual mind and body. Light and darkness, birth and death, and all the other pairs of opposites, such as joy and sorrow, are the result of ignorance.

The wise see only one pure consciousness—Brahman. The greatest of all wonders on the earth is that the Infinite lives in the finite vessel and the same Infinite dwells in the finite universe. It is His delight; it is His majesty; it is His splendor. When the aspirant knows the Truth and realizes the Self, the aspirant is free from all bondage and attains final liberation or emancipation.

Here ends the second canto of Chapter 2.

Chapter
3

Mundaka
Upanishad

CANTO 1

VERSE 1:

Two identical birds that are eternal companions perch
in the very same tree. One eats many fruits of various
tastes. The other only witnesses without eating.

With the help of a beautiful metaphor, this verse illustrates
the difference between jivatman, the individual soul, and paramatman, or absolute Brahman, so that the aspirant can easily
understand. Essentially and qualitatively, they are one and the
same, but the human mind needs a clear explanation regarding
these two words. The verse describes two birds that have beautiful wings. They are very close to each other in friendship; like
the twin laws of life, they are inseparable. They both perch on
the same branch of the same tree of life.

According to the non-dualistic school of philosophy, the
center of consciousness is that force from which consciousness
flows in different degrees and grades. However, because of the
apparent superimposition, the being is bound by the body and

mind and develops attachments to objects, performs actions, and reaps the fruits therein. Ishvara, or God, is pure consciousness conditioned by the cosmic power of the Absolute Brahman, also called maya. It is devoid of avidya or ignorance. It is eternal, brilliant, and omniscient.

A few scholars think that the description of the two birds refers to the mind and jivatman. But the other bird is pure Consciousness, absolutely unaffected by the taint of enjoyment and suffering. The individual soul is an image of the parambrahman, reflected on the lake of the mind. Just as the sun and its image are inseparable, so also are the jivatman and paramatman actually one and the same, and thus, inseparable. The individual soul identifies itself with the objects of the mind and body and feels itself to be the doer of all actions. However, this is the influence of the mind, which is merely the instrument of the jiva through which the jiva feels the pairs of opposites, such as enjoyment of the fruits of actions and the experiences of pain and pleasure, or grief and sorrow.

In the *Bhagavad Gita,* which is derived from Upanishadic literature, the pairs of opposites—such as pain and pleasure— are felt when the mind, with the help of its senses, contacts the objects of the world. In such a case, two kinds of sensations can be received—one is called pain, the other is pleasure.

The body is understood as the tree, whose roots have grown out of Brahman, like the whole universe that rises from Brahman. The students of the school of duality and qualified non-duality believe that jiva is an entirely separate entity and enjoys the fruits of actions. However, according to the Advaitins, non-dual philosophers, the individual soul, being spirit, can never undergo any change. The superimpositions *(anyonya bhasa)* make one feel that jiva, the individual soul, has an identity separate from pure consciousness or Brahman. Mind and matter experience various changes and modifications, but the soul itself never changes. Being spirit, it cannot experience modification. It witnesses and remains unaffected by the functions and modifications of the mind.

Only the knowledge of Brahman or paravidya is able to help the aspirant realize the Absolute Truth. This knowledge destroys the superimpositions on Reality with the help of practical disciplines, as is explained in previous chapters, by the metaphor of the bow and arrow and the target. This chapter deals with the subject of the spiritual disciplines, such as truthfulness of speech, the practice of meditation through focusing the mind on atman alone, and the performance of selfless actions.

The aspirant then attains freedom from the sufferings that the individual soul feels. The individual soul refers to the spirit or atman, possessing the vehicle of the unconscious mind, which is the reservoir of all impressions, thoughts, feelings, and desires. As long as an individual soul—pure spirit—is using the vehicle, it is called jivatman. We can also put it this way: when an aspirant perceives the individual soul while still using the vehicle of the unconscious mind, that entity is called jivatman. When the aspirant perceives pure Consciousness without the imposition of the vehicle—the unconscious mind—then he perceives pure Consciousness or atman. This imposition is destroyed when the aspirant establishes himself in the true nature of atman without any such superimposition.

VERSE 2:

> *Seated in the same tree, the deluded purusha*
> *becomes entangled and worries helplessly.*

*However, the moment it recognizes the glory and
greatness of the other bird, it attains freedom from
all pain and misery.*

The second verse makes the aspirant aware that the two
beautiful winged birds are the individual soul and pure consciousness without any superimposition of individuality. Two
feelings lurk in the human mind as a result of the absence of
pure knowledge. The individual soul is bewildered because of
its own impotence, which is self-acquired through its identifica-
tion with the objects of the mind, which are constantly changing and decaying.

Under the heavy, self-imposed weight of ignorance, desire,
action, and the longing to reap the fruits of action, the individual soul is drowned in the ocean of samsara. Suppose a swimmer
reverses the correct technique of paddling with his hands: if,
rather than propelling his hands away from his body, and thus
pushing himself forward, he instead pulls the water in toward
him, he will drown. As long as the individual soul does not yet
have the knowledge of how to renounce and destroy all its fetters and how to take delight in that renunciation, he cannot
cross the mire of delusion created by the ocean of samsara.

When the same swimmer or aspirant knows and practices
the techniques of *tyaga* and *vairagya,* he gains freedom from
the fetters created by the superimpositions of his own creation.
False identifications change a personality. The word "personality" Comes from the root, *persona,* a Greek word meaning
"a mask" and the process of playing a role in a theater. These
masks create different personalities. An individual soul wears
a particular mask according to its predispositions and then
regards itself as a son, grandson, wife, husband, or friend. He

creates attachments for himself and a completely new personality. Thus, individuality is formed and he forgets his true nature. Then he experiences the pairs of opposites—pain and pleasure, joy and sorrow. Such individuality also makes him or her experience birth and death. When, with the help of spiritual disciplines, the aspirant realizes that all these relationships in the external world are self-created and reestablishes himself in his true nature, he attains freedom.

The individual soul creates the whirlpool for himself, as well as the numerous troubles and perplexities in external life, which are actually the faces of ignorance. In this state, one becomes helpless and impotent. One loses self-confidence, and although he has every possible power and means, he feels that he is powerless and experiences a series of self-condemning thoughts. When the aspirant analyzes and distills the whole philosophy of life, he finds that his suffering is due to maya, under whose influence he has forgotten his true nature and has begun identifying himself with the objects of the world.

When the aspirant develops a longing for spiritual life instead of worldly objects, and when he or she practices disciplines such as non-violence, truthfulness, and continence, as explained by Patanjali, the codifier of Yoga science, then the aspirant attains a new spirit of self-control and a tranquil mind. He or she is able to contemplate and meditate. The Inner Dweller, who resides in the human body, remains unaffected by grief and sorrow, pain and pleasure, hunger and thirst, and old age and death. All these changes are deep-rooted habits of the body, and not of the Inner Dweller. When the aspirant turns his mind and looks within, he becomes aware of the bird who is witnessing. Then he finds that it is he who is responsible for his own suffering. It is also he who can destroy the fetters of ignorance and thus become free, regaining the status of that bird who resides in the body with complete freedom.

VERSE 3:

> *When the aspirant realizes purusha, the*
> *consciousness that is self-effulgent, the true force*
> *behind all actions, the Lord and source of knowledge,*
> *then such a wise seeker washes off the samskaras of*
> *all virtuous and non-virtuous deeds, becomes pure,*
> *and attains the highest state of equanimity.*

This third verse reiterates that when the aspirant learns to contemplate and meditate on "the golden hue," then he or she enjoys the splendid happiness of the limitless and immutable Brahman. Freedom from duality means the unification of the individual soul with Brahman. The aspirant, therefore, should tread the path of spiritual practice with firm determination and develop an intense longing—not a longing for the world or to enjoy worldly pleasures, but only to attain absolute freedom. He can accomplish such a task in this lifetime. Hail to the teachings of the Upanishads, which have the power to convert an impotent one into a valiant one! Such a great one knows how to live in the world and remain eternally delighted, by enjoying the immortal fruits of renouncing worldly pleasures.

VERSE 4:

> *Knowing the truth that it is prana that shines*
> *through all living beings, a realized yogi*
> *takes no interest in pedantic discussions and*
> *debates. Rather he delights in atman, enjoys his*

meditation, and is considered to be the highest of
the knowers of Brahman.

In this verse, the word *prana* has been used for the first unit of life, which is an eternal wave that has arisen from the ocean of bliss. It can be called the supreme being, too, for this is the very first wave of light that creates many ripples, such as the mind, its modifications, the senses, and the various elements of the body. Here, the word *prana* is not meant for the two breaths that constantly guard the city of life. The advanced student of the sovereign science of the Upanishads knows that the breath is like a horse and the rider is prana. One is only a vehicle; the other is the rider.

Pranayama is the science of learning that all the phases of life are the projections of this eternal wave, which is called prana. It is not inert or inanimate, but it is the center of Consciousness within, the first manifested one, the dweller in the cave of the heart, as has been previously explained.

There are three paths of sadhana; First, sadhana through the mind, intellect, and emotion, which is the path of knowledge and bhakti; second, sadhana through brahmacharya, which means austerity and control of the senses through celibacy or walking in Brahman-consciousness all the time; and third, the path of *vayu*, which does not merely mean breathing exercises. These exercises help to regulate the motion of the lungs and keep the body healthy. By regulating the motion of the lungs, the body becomes a fit instrument for sadhana, and not an obstacle on the path of self-realization. All breathing exercises are valid, but the advanced students know that the first unit of life is really called prana. Because of its support, the mind functions intelligently and brilliantly, and the senses have the power to see, hear, taste, touch, and smell. Therefore, the light that shines forth comes from the origin—prana. This light is the light of brilliance and intelligence. This resides within the human body.

VERSE 5:

> *This atman can he experienced through constant practice of Truth, tapas, right knowledge, and brahmacharya. Yogis devoid of all impurities see this self-illumined, bright light within this very body.*

This verse hands over to the advanced student, who has determined to tread the path of light, the keys of the keyless gates of the Kingdom of God. The Kingdom of God lies within. We have already explained that to reach the last gate requires sincere effort and cultivation of truthfulness, austerity, right knowledge, and continence. These practices purify the way of the soul, and then the resplendent light of atman dawns.

Repeatedly, the Upanishadic verses remind the aspirant to follow the path of contemplation and meditation. The seer of Upanishadic wisdom has already explained many times that the Supreme Self resides within the heart of all beings and at the same time dwells in the universe. Knowledge dwells in the universe, but to "reside in the inner chamber" is different—a practical and direct way of knowing the Truth, which is hinted at.

There are several guidelines to follow if you want to learn how to meditate: first, you need to set a time for meditation and contemplation, and during that time, you should not be disturbed in any way. Second, a quiet and calm corner of the house is needed for meditation. Third, the issues of time, place, and posture play important roles in the path of meditation.

When you pose for meditation, you should learn to sit

in an erect position, keeping the head, neck, and trunk in a straight line, without tension. One should physically relax his body and still it. When the body is stilled, a joy of a minor degree is experienced.

Breathing exercises help you attain serenity of breath. To create serenity of the breath there should not be any noise, jerkiness, or shallowness. This stillness of breath can be attained with simple effort after one learns to practice diaphragmatic breathing. Other exercises, such as channel purification, and internal and external retention, practiced under the guidance of a competent teacher, also become helpful in attaining serenity in the breath. Then, the aspirant learns how to deal with the thoughts coming forward from the storehouse of merits and demerits, known as the unconscious mind. The aspirant is instructed to become the witness and not get involved in analyzing or identifying himself with the pleasantness or unpleasantness of his thoughts.

Eventually, a time comes when the aspirant starts to enjoy the delight of being a seer, and then the mind and its thoughts and feelings do not disturb him. Such a state of mind leads the student to experience silence. This is a living silence; by experiencing this silence, the aspirant is immensely benefited, both physically and mentally. Meditation heals both body and mind. A simple, systematic method of fathoming the inner realms patiently and persistently, under the guidance of a teacher of meditation, will help an aspirant to enjoy inner serenity and peace.

In this process, the mind becomes purified, just as gold is purified when it is heated. Such a mind becomes like a calm lake, and then one can see what is under the surface of the water. There lies the glittering, immortal jewel of atman. After reaching this state, a student attains a deeper state of silence, known as samadhi. It is according to this practice that the habits of body and mind, which are conditioned by time, are dropped. Then consciousness is expanded, and the same consciousness remains all the time.

Upanishadic prayers and the contemplation of the mahavakyas, the great sayings, deepen the inner awareness of the aspirant. Therefore, prayer and contemplation are auxiliary to meditation.

The aspirant should not stop practicing this inward method and should not become involved in so-called *siddhis,* or supernatural experiences, which he may have while treading the path of spirituality. Not all miracles remain miracles once you understand them.

Sense perception is limited. The field of the conscious mind, though higher, is also still limited. The field of the unconscious mind, though vast, is like a dense forest, and one cannot go beyond it without the help of a competent teacher and meditative practice, conducted regularly and punctually.

VERSE 6:

> *Truth alone wins, never untruth. The path leading to the Divine is paved by Truth. By following this path, the seers who are free from all desires attain the highest abode of Truth.*

The first line of this verse is often quoted by speakers and writers for their own convenience, but if someone practices truth with mind, action, and speech, he or she becomes victorious. One who leads the life of spiritual striving and understands that practicing truth is the most important part of the discipline attains the opportunity to tread the path of light or devayana, "the path of bright beings." Such aspirants attain liberation after casting off their bodies.

The eighteenth mantra of the *Ishopanishad* explains the path of light. To learn to practice Truth, it is important to learn to bring principles into practice. One should first learn not to lie. Not lying means not to speak words or sentences that do not relate exactly to the world of objects. By practicing not to lie, one speaks Truth. Thus, applying the principle of speaking Truth means *do not lie*. When the student learns to use the principles laid down by the Upanishads in his practical life, then the whole structure of the verse changes. Therefore, nonlying leads one to Truth. The verse also hints at the way a student should learn to direct his or her speech. Practicing truthfulness with mind, action, and speech is a complete practice. Then, the student learns to refrain from doing what is not to be done. He learns what is not to be thought and does not speak that which is not to be spoken. By not speaking, thinking, or doing what is wrong, one starts thinking, speaking, and doing what is right. Therefore, all the rules and injunctions declared in the scriptures are practiced this way. It is important to be aware that principles and practices are two different things. Aspirants who are free from delusion, falsehood, vanity, and attachment to the world and who have no worldly desires attain this supreme state.

VERSE 7:

> *It is infinite, divine, and indescribable, and is subtler than the subtlest. It is further than the farthest, yet to those who see It, It is very close, residing in the cave of the heart.*

This verse uses the word *vast* to describe the experience of happiness and delight, which is as vast as imagination, which is subtler than the most subtle and self-luminous. Verily, the glimpse of the supreme Self, Brahman, leads the aspirant to self-realization. Then he or she knows the One who is far and yet very near and knows that the same One is the indweller in all human beings and all creatures.

He directly realizes that the Truth leads him to the experience of that knowledge which is self-luminous, like the sun, moon, and stars. This knowledge is subtler than *akasha* or space. The wise thus identify themselves as seers and see in all living beings the same Self of all.

VERSE 8:

> *It cannot be seen with the eyes, nor described with speech; It cannot be known through the senses or achieved through austerities or rituals and ceremonies. When, as a result of knowledge, his mind is purified and calm, the yogi meditating on the Absolute attains the direct experience.*

This verse again gives a special method of realizing Brahman. This great and bold saying should not be misunderstood. I will ask the reader to enjoy a humorous story before considering it.

Once, I met a Mohammedan, a good and gentle man, but poor in his knowledge of the *Koran Sarif.* I asked him, "Do you attend your *namaz,* prayers, regularly?" He said, "It is written in the Koran: 'Don't read namaz,' so I don't read the Koran and I don't do my prayers."

This shocked me, and I said, "Can you show me where that is written?" He brought out the holy book, which was wrapped in a blue silken scarf, and he opened the book and showed me the verse. It said, "Don't read the Koran." Showing me only that passage, he immediately closed the book.

I said, "Please open the book and show me what is written beyond that verse." It actually said: "Don't read the Koran when you are impure or unclean."

Thus, the shallow study of the scriptures or the mere study of the scriptures without practicing spiritual disciplines will not allow the student to go beyond the spheres of the sun and moon. Mere knowledge of the scriptures will nourish only the vanity and therefore the so-called "learned ones" will become only egotistical rather than actual knowers of the valuable sayings of the scriptures. Such is the case with people who do philanthropic or charitable work for the sake of name and fame, because their lust, the real motivation behind their charity, will not change their internal states of mind. Therefore, the verse says, even knowledge of the scriptures and charitable work do not help one to dispel the darkness of ignorance. But this does not mean that one should not study scriptures or do charitable work.

This verse says that sensory perception has no power to grasp Brahman, nor does penance, nor even philanthropic or charitable works. If someone does not understand the saying correctly, he will not grasp its true meaning. It means that those vain and proud people, who consider themselves well-versed in the sayings of the Upanishads, cannot realize Brahman. Those who do not have inner strength and awareness of atman, or those whose intellect is sharpened but trained in understanding only the external world alone, can never attain the kingdom of Brahman.

Even the best of actions, such as doing charitable works, will not satisfy the inner longing if such actions are done for name and fame or to satisfy one's own egotistical whims. Therefore, the verse explains that the mere knowledge of scriptures and charitable deeds performed in the world have no power to lead the aspirant on the path of spirituality.

Buddhi is the finest of all modifications of our internal states. It is indeed a great instrument of knowledge. By virtue of its own nature, it is pure. If we do not throw pebbles in the lake, the water of the lake remains calm, and then one can easily see what is at the bottom of the lake. But if one goes on throwing pebbles into the lake, then the ripples arising in the lake will obstruct the aspirant from being able to see what is at the bottom. The lake of mind is polluted by the selfish desires and attachments to the world.

Thus, buddhi is not aware of Brahman. However, when pebbles are not thrown into the lake of mind—when many desires, thoughts, feelings, and inclinations do not create ripples in the lake of the mind—then it remains calm and serene. Through the pure and higher buddhi, one realizes and expands awareness.

VERSE 9:

> *This extremely subtle atman, residing in the cave of the heart, can be known through pure intelligence. Prana has entered this body in five forms. Along with prana, mind pervades the whole body of living beings. When this body-mind organization is purified, atman shines forth.*

The method of self-purification, especially purification of buddhi, is explained here. In the previous verse, we briefly described a systematic method of meditation and mentioned the necessity of contemplation and prayer. But in this verse, the meaning is somewhat different. The path of pure intellect means the path of jnana. This word is exploited by modern teachers; they do what they want, and they teach without direct experience, calling themselves jnanis. The path of jnana is like walking on a razor's edge; it is possible only when an aspirant purifies the higher buddhi. Higher buddhi has inherent qualities of perfectness and exactness in knowing what is right or wrong, what is permanent or impermanent, mortal or immortal. It knows how to make decisions on time, as well as how to judge the objects of the world without identifying with them.

When the intellect is purified by listening to the sayings of the great scriptures and then pondering and contemplating the gist of those sayings, it leads the aspirant of this path to the state of *sakshatkara,* which means "seeing Truth face-to-face." The atman is realized within the human body and is discriminated from the first unit of the life force and its vehicles, which are many, although in this scripture only five are mentioned.

On the path of jnana yoga, buddhi, which is the finest instrument of knowledge, is purified directly. The purification practices consist of methods of consciously withdrawing buddhi from the sense perceptions and conceptualization of manas, with which it is interwoven in every human being. Most aspirants of this path think that jnana yoga allows one to do, speak, or act in any way they want; this is not true. The purification exercises for higher buddhi are very subtle, and only a fortunate few can tread this path and attain success.

VERSE 10:

> *A person with a purified mind can attain*
> *any plane of existence or any object of desire.*
> *Therefore, anyone desiring to be prosperous*
> *should honor and serve the knower of atman.*

The tenth verse provides a very subtle insight for all aspirants who are treading the path of self-realization, whether it is a path of selfless action, love and devotion, *raja yoga,* or jnana yoga. In all these paths, the purification of internal states is essential. Purification of the desires is very important. Whatever object the aspirant fixes his mind and heart upon, whatever becomes the object of meditation, the aspirant attains those words or objects. Many students do japa, but during the time they are doing japa, their mind continuously broods on the forms of the objects of the world. When that occurs, then the japa becomes mere recitation. Therefore, Patanjali, the codifier of yoga science, says: *"Tad japas tadartha bhavanam—*The japa practice is complete in itself, provided it is done with knowledge and with full devotion."

Then real japa begins when japa becomes *ajapa japa,* when all modifications of the mind are purified, and when the totality of the mind is unified and becomes one-pointed. Then, japa goes on unconsciously all the time, even during sleep.

Those who have studied Chaitanya Mahaprabhu's literature will know that even during sleep, he used to inhale and exhale his mantra, and anybody seated in that room could clearly hear his mantra constantly recited with every breath of his life. When the aspirant breathes mantra, eats mantra, sleeps mantra, and walks mantra, then such a practice leads him to the highest and direct experience of the self-luminous atman.

This verse describes the fact that such a great sage's presence will bless anyone and everyone, and that his *darshana* will lead the people of the world toward prosperity. Hail to those self-realized beings! Let us pay homage to those great ones!

Here ends the first canto of Chapter 3.

CANTO 2

VERSE 1:

*Knowers of the supreme Brahman know that the
whole universe is supported by Brahman and shines
through the light of Brahman. Those who remove
all worldly desires and worship purusha, pure
consciousness, transcend the cycle of birth and death.*

The previous verse said that if the aspirant worships while
having worldly motives, then he or she attains success in the
world, but not on the path of spirituality. This is called *sakama
puja,* worship with a desire. However, this verse says that worship without worldly motives and purely for spiritual enlightenment is a means to liberation.

A person of self-realization, alone, knows the Supreme
Brahman, One without a second. The wise, who completely
devote their time and life to self-realization attain emancipation
and are free from the changes of death and birth.

There cannot be any delusion or sorrow for that wise one who has realized the unity in diversity, his own self in the Self of all. He hates none and loves all. The aspirant is delightfully confronted with the consequences of the idea that his infinite Self is his true nature, the true nature of every man and woman. One who has realized atman and perceives that same atman in all beings, how can he or she be separate from others? Then who can hate whom? The Self is one with all, and the only life expression of this vision is universal love. Love is a binding force that is life, while separateness comes from hatred. Love is one of the highest points of human excellence.

Human society collectively longs to attain this state of civilization. Alas, such great people are rare, although they exist in all traditions and cultures. But if all the societies of the world produced such people who could emanate love selflessly to all, then human beings would never have a longing to go to heaven, for all the heavenly joys—even the immortal joy of Brahman—would be attained here and now in this lifetime. Where are those prophets of love? It is not the intellect, but the heart that will transform human society.

Grief and delusion come to a human being when he identifies himself with his limited body, mind, and its objects. When one identifies oneself with the non-Self aspect of his personality, he is weak and helpless and commits many mistakes and experiences tension, grief, and sorrow. The illusion of separateness has a critical, constricting effect on the growth of the human mind, intellect, and society.

Jesus says, "Love thy neighbor as thyself." The Upanishads say, "The whole universe is your family and all the members of the universe are your family members." The purpose of spirituality is to destroy the illusion of separateness. A river cut off from its mainstream must become stagnant; so too is the case when man cuts himself off from the mainstream, atman. Then he falls into sorrow, grief, and delusion.

VERSE 2:

> *By contrast, those who do not renounce all desires are pulled by their worldly desires and are born again and again amidst those very surroundings they desire. But for one whose desires are fulfilled and who is established in the Self, all desires vanish in this lifetime.*

This verse repeats the same idea expressed in the previous verse. For those who long to enjoy the objects of desire and constantly brood about them, their own desire becomes the cause for their rebirth. It is actually the unfulfilled desires that prompt the individual soul to be reborn on the earth. Among all desires, the desire of attachment is the one most responsible for rebirth. Suppose that someone is dying but has an intense desire in the mind, and that desire has not been fulfilled in this lifetime: such a desire becomes the reason for the individual soul to come again to this earth, so that the unfulfilled desire is fulfilled.

When the sage sincerely treads the path of spirituality and has no attachments or worldly desires, but only a single desire to attain Brahman—even if he does not attain Brahman in this lifetime—that one desire for self-realization or the attainment of Brahman will motivate him to again follow the path that he has trodden before. The wise, therefore, with all their resources and spiritual disciplines, destroy the fetters of ignorance and attain perfection in this lifetime.

VERSE 3:

> *The knowledge of atman cannot be attained*
> *through discourse, intellectual analysis, or even*
> *extensive study, but only to those whom it chooses*
> *does atman unfold itself.*

On the path of self-realization, when all efforts and spiritual disciplines are successfully practiced by the aspirant, a point is attained when there is no desire at all. But this state is attained by the aspirants or wise ones who long intensely, with their whole hearts and minds. To them, the luminous atman reveals itself and its own nature—that which is peace, happiness, and bliss.

Spiritual discipline removes the veil created by ignorance. True longing to attain Brahman possesses the power to do it. The Self is already there; it is neither imported nor transported from any plane, but it is the innermost being within. It only reveals itself when the aspirant has accomplished his or her spiritual sadhana by purifying the mind, intellect, and heart.

Here the doctrine of grace is intended to play a great role in the life of an aspirant. The aspirant should understand that atman is not attainable through mere learning or discourses, nor through intellectual gymnastics. It is attained only by those who are chosen; it is a law that similar chooses similar.

When an aspirant lifts himself and his sadhana from the physical to the mental, and finally from the mental to the spiritual, then he stands face-to-face in front of atman, wanting to be one with his immortal Self. To such an aspirant, atman reveals its true nature.

VERSE 4:

This atman cannot be attained by those who lack inner strength, sincerity, tapas, or dispassion. However, one who is endowed with these means attains Self-Realization and as a result, enters the realm of Brahman.

This verse forcefully explains to the aspirant that strength is the first capacity to be regained, for inner strength is robbed by the mind and the sense pleasures, and the aspirant should be careful to guard his inner strength exactly the way someone does when they light a little candle flame and try to protect it from the breeze. The same little light can eventually grow into a forest conflagration.

In such a case, all the adverse circumstances lose their negative value and, instead of creating obstacles, they start to help the aspirant to unfold the inner dimensions of life. But students who are destitute of strength cannot attain; they need inner strength and determination first. Serious obstacles are created by *pramada*—inertia, laziness, and carelessness. These are the prime enemies of a sadhaka, which obscure the vision of the splendid, self-illumined atman.

But the wise ones build their inner strength by practicing self-discipline and determination. They strive with full vigor and a one-pointed mind, and finally they attain union with Brahman. Without yoking the individual self with the cosmic Self or Brahman, practicing a spiritual discipline without a definite system cannot lead one to attain the goal of life. False austerity or mortifications are not helpful.

VERSE 5:

> *Upon attaining this, seers become content in*
> *their wisdom, established in atman, free from*
> *attachment and desire, and fully at peace. Upon*
> *attaining the all-pervading consciousness, the*
> *realized souls enter the realm of Brahman!*

The sages become content after the knowledge of self-realization. They are firmly established in the supreme bliss, free from attachments and passions. Such calm and tranquil souls, completely devoted to atman, ultimately become One, exactly the way a river becomes one with the ocean.

Brahman is pure Consciousness. Individuality exists through the association with the body, senses, and mind, which constantly feed the ego. The ego separates the individual from the whole by creating a wall. This is all illusory, but the human being thinks that it is permanent and real.

When a mirror is thickly enveloped by dust, one cannot see one's face in such a mirror. But when the dust is washed off, one can see one's own face in the mirror. Such superimpositions are false and can be washed off with spiritual practice. The knowledge of the real Self washes off all the accumulated dust of the impure mind. Knowledge of atman alone leads one to self-realization. Such a sage merges into Brahman after casting off his body.

VERSE 6:

> *Those who attain the final, precise wisdom*
> *expounded in Vedanta and who, by following the*
> *path of renunciation, have purified their minds,*
> *attain freedom from all bondage, and after casting*

***off the body, go to the realm of Brahman, the realm
of highest immortality.***

The same idea is reiterated in this verse. The renunciates should know that even after purifying all the stains of avidya from the heart, mind, and buddhi, the vague impressions of ignorance still remain, although the seeker's view of them is obscured. It is exactly like when you do a wonderful job of cleaning your living room and think that your room looks immaculate; then one day, you lift the carpet and are shocked and amazed to see how much dust remains hidden under the carpet. Therefore, the wise ones form a strong habit of going into deep meditation and not allowing the dust of ignorance to accumulate or to touch their internal state.

Such a wise person is an illumined soul and attains freedom from maya. All the impositions and limitations created by time, space, and causality are destroyed, for he or she realizes oneness with Brahman. Then the wise one transports himself to the transcendent Reality, not the reality of the relative plane, but the Reality that is self-existent. It is the source of all Consciousness, without beginning or end.

Therefore, such an enlightened one does not return to the relative planes of the universe. Of his death the poets say, "the day of parting is actually the day of meeting." When the individual soul is wedded with the Absolute, such a bliss is inexplicable, unimaginable, and immeasurable.

His ego is totally annihilated. Here, there is a subtle point to be understood: what happens to him? Does he become non-existent? The answer is, certainly not. He becomes one with the self-existent Bliss Absolute. Such a wise person does not leave footprints behind to be traced. Just as a bird flies through the air without leaving any trace, so, likewise, does the individual soul fly from this shore of life to the other shore of life without leaving a trace. Not leaving the trace of a footprint means not leaving any samskaras unburned in the fire of knowledge.

VERSE 7:

> *At the time of liberation, all the fifteen constituents of the body (five gross elements, five senses, and five pranas) return to their sources. The senses subside in their origins. All previous karmas, intellectual knowledge, and the individual soul— all become one with Absolute Brahman.*

This verse satisfies the curiosity of the sadhaka by describing what happens to the body, senses, and mind after death. The question arises, what happens to the body, breath, senses, and mind when the immortal bird takes off into the space of bliss and meets her beloved Supreme Lord and becomes inseparably one, never to return?

The *Prashna Upanishad* and the *Mundaka Upanishad* are similar in their teachings and as we said, they come from the same source—*Atharva Veda.* By considering this metaphor you can understand what happens to the human body after the bird has flown to her final destination. Place a jar full of water in front of the sun and then break it any way you want. The water finds its own level and meets water. The outer covering of the jar meets its source, earth, and the space of the jar meets space. The reflection of the sun meets the sun. All the components of either the jar or the body meet or merge back into their respective sources.

Actually, no one dies; the sense organs go back to their cosmic source. The organs of hearing go to subtle akasha, the organ of touch to vayu, and the organ of vision to fire. The individual soul willfully assumes, because of its desires, body after body until the attainment of liberation is accomplished.

The highest, immutable, and imperishable "sky" is birthless, deathless, and therefore there is no destruction. When the clouds are removed, then the sun reveals itself.

VERSE 8:

> *Just as flowing rivers give up their names and forms*
> *and merge into the ocean, so does the realized soul*
> *disidentify itself from all names and forms and*
> *attain the highest and self-illumined purusha.*

This verse inspires the aspirant, "May you flow like a river that dances and sings the songs of the eternal, while traveling along many, many bends in the riverbed until she finally meets her beloved ocean. May you learn to allow the flow of the life-force without creating dams of stagnant water, which become a source of illness and disease."

That is why true sannyasins, renunciates, move all the time, or, whenever they sit, their journey is called journey without movement. They move not, yet they go ahead. Such individual souls, who have become one with Brahman, do not suffer on account of the pangs of separation.

VERSE 9:

> *One who knows Brahman verily becomes*
> *Brahman, and in his lineage, no one remains*
> *ignorant of Brahman. He goes beyond all sorrow*
> *and vice and attains freedom from all the knots at*

the cave of the heart, and thus, becomes immortal.

This verse says that he who has realized Brahman and has become one with Brahman is verily Brahman. Anyone who comes into his presence becomes elevated by his subtle, spiritual vibrations. No member of the family in which he dwells remains ignorant, because he becomes the example.

Let me tell you that the presence of a great sage can teach the aspirant without words. Advanced disciples are taught by their gurus from a long distance. It is also true that the best of the teachings are imparted in silence through silence.

When the body is still and the mind is perfectly tranquil, in such silence, the mind has no questions, and if there are no questions, then such a mind does not need answers. A long and close association with a truly spiritual leader is able to establish a relationship between the preceptor and pupil that is higher than any other relationship on the earth. Just as a newborn baby's babbling is clearly understood by its mother and the mother's language clearly understood by the infant, so the words spoken by the guru in the voice of silence are clearly understood by his close disciples, provided the guru remains a transmitter and the disciple a receiver.

Another interesting question arises: then, in which language can the mind continue to jabber, because it has forgotten all its languages? The answer is that it is one with the bliss, exactly as a drop of water becomes one with the ocean.

VERSE 10:

As is said in the mantra: this knowledge of Brahman should be imparted only to those who are sincere, studious, inclined toward Brahman,

self-disciplined, who are dedicated to one seer,
and who have taken a vow of carrying fire on their
heads according to the rules.

According to the sovereign science of the *Rig Veda,* a guideline has been set down for the preceptor, which pertains to imparting the knowledge of the Vedas and Upanishads. It is said that it is imparted only to those who have performed their duties and who are well- versed in the scriptural knowledge, are fully devoted to Brahman, who have firm faith, and have offered all that they think is theirs in the *ekarshi* fire. The word *ekarshi* here has been used for the fire of knowledge, which completely burns the impurities and liberates one from ignorance.

There is another system introduced and discussed in this verse. In previous verses, the paths of enlightenment through meditation and devotion have been discussed. The path of enlightenment through jnana has also been described, but the path of enlightenment through action has not yet been explained.

This verse seems to be devoted to selfless action performed skillfully. The law of karma is inevitable, and without performing one's duties and actions, the heart, mind, intellect, emotions, thoughts, and all aspects of buddhi cannot be purified. Understanding this cultivates a proper atmosphere that enables a sadhaka to do sadhana with vigor and delight.

A seeker of truth first has to have a profound knowledge of the Vedas. Patanjali, the codifier of Yoga Science, says that it is not the words that are eternal, but the knowledge contained therein that is eternal, impersonal, and imperishable. Therefore, these scriptures are superb containers of knowledge and furnish the essential means for gaining self-realization.

In the primary state, an aspirant worships Brahman with full devotion and love, but it is Brahman with attributes, because the mind is still being prepared to be tranquil. Finally, pure consciousness is attained.

A seeker of truth should have faith in his spiritual preceptor and in the sayings of the great books, as well as the sayings of the great sages. *Svadhyaya* is another important factor that acts like a fuel to make the fire blaze. Without faith, the mind refuses to meditate. Faith should be cherished.

There is a mention of the sacrifice called *ekarshi.* Symbolically, one is required to carry fire on one's head. This is described in the . By this means, an aspirant acquires good concentration of mind and purity of heart.

Such concentration is like that of a woman who daily fetches water from the plazas that are outside villages in India. With the water vessel on her head, she dances and sings and discusses all the things she wants with her friends, but her attention remains on her vessel. So also should be the case with the people of the world, who are mostly karma yogis. They should learn to do their duties, but their attention should be constantly on the center of consciousness within themselves. This awareness should be cultivated.

A man in the world cannot liberate himself from the bondage of karma without performing completely selfless actions. So, similarly, does a renunciate purify his heart and mind through tapas (austerity), svadhyaya (study of scriptures), and *Ishvara pranidhana* (surrender of himself to the Lord alone).

There is always a difference between these disciplines and actions performed in the external world. These disciplines do not have a binding effect, but instead furnish the means and inspire the aspirant on the path of sadhana.

VERSE 11:

> *The seer Angiras explained Truth in ancient times.*
> *A person who has fulfilled his vows may study this*
> *Upanishad. Homage to the great sages! Homage to*
> *the great sages!*

The seer Angiras taught this truth in ancient times and declares that this scripture should not be read by those who have not taken vows: that is, by those who do not have determination to practice a spiritual discipline, as given by the teacher. It is clear that the knowledge of Brahman should not be given to an impure person.

The study of the sovereign science needs a well-equipped lab. If the lab is not fully equipped—meaning if the functioning of the body, breath, and mind are not coordinated in the lab of the human body—then a person will be making a futile effort and wasting his time and energy.

The great sages are realized ones and have become the channels through whom pure knowledge flows. Such sages transmit this knowledge to those aspirants who are fully determined to purify themselves, those who are in the process of purifying themselves, or those fortunate few who have already purified their internal states.

The word *homage* or salutation is repeated twice to express the feeling of gratitude and reverence toward the sages who teach the sovereign science of Brahman.

Here ends the second canto of Chapter 3.

Glossary

addhvaryu: One of three priests designated in the Vedas to perform ceremonies. The role of the addhvaryu is to arrange the physical aspects of the ceremony—the articles used, as well as the site.

advaita: Non-dual; without a second. This refers to the Absolute Brahman or the Vedic philosophy that expounds the theory of non-dual Brahman.

agamin karma: There are three aspects or effects of karma called prarabdha, sancita and agamin. Agamin refers to the karma that will come to fruition in future lives.

agni: Fire. There are many meanings of the word agni, or fire, forty of which are most prominent. Depending on context, agni means a Brahmin; a man of wisdom; the fire of light; life breath; prana; heat; leader.

agnihotra: Fire ceremony; fire offering. The true meaning of agnihotra is that in the fire of life, oblations are constantly offered.

ahamkara: Loosely translated as ego; together, manas, buddhi, and ahamkara comprise the inner instrument known as *antahakarana.* It is through this inner faculty that one identifies oneself with the objects of the world, such as "I am this body" or "That is my chair." More strictly, in Sankhya and Yoga philosophy it is the "I-maker." It refers to a function of mind through which pure consciousness, purusha, falsely identifies itself with non-self, material objects.

ajapa japa: Japa without japa; the spontaneous and constant awareness of one's mantra; constant awareness of one's mantra with every breath of life.

ajna chakra: The center between the eyebrows; the seat of mind; the center of consciousness that receives the wisdom from the higher chakra, sahasrara.

akasha: Space; one of the five tattvas or gross elements (earth, water, fire, air, and space).

anahata chakra: The heart center, associated with the air element; the center located between the upper and lower hemispheres of the body, in the region of the heart. Students of the Mishra school of Tantra perform their mental worship at this chakra.

ananda: Joy. There are two kinds of ananda, or joy, that a human being can experience: one is sensual joy, which is experienced by ordinary human beings; it lasts only for a short time and creates a desire for repetition. The other joy is the highest of joys—everlasting unity with Brahman.

anandamaya kosha: The sheath of bliss; one of the five sheaths, or koshas, that cover the effulgent Brahman or atman.

annum: Food or the essence of food; life sustaining energy.

annamaya kosha: The food sheath, the physical body that is nourished by and grows on food; one of the five sheaths, or koshas, that cover the effulgent Brahman or atman.

anyonya bhasa: The superimpositions that make jiva, individual soul, feel that it has an identity separate from pure consciousness or Brahman.

apana: Downward moving pranic force; function of prana that tends to move downward. Also identified with exhalation.

apara vidya: Lower knowledge, the knowledge of lower reality or the manifest world, in contrast to para vidya, the knowledge of Brahman. Apara vidya includes all of the mundane arts and sciences.

Atharva Veda: The fourth book of the Vedas which, in addition to spiritual wisdom, also focuses on modern sciences; the source of the *Mundaka Upanishad.*

atman: Pure Consciousness, the pure Self, the unchanging, eternal Truth that is beyond the entire manifest world.

AUM: Sound that represents the Absolute Brahman. According to the Upanishads, the word *AUM* consists of three letters— A, U, and M—representing waking, dreaming, and deep sleep. After the word *AUM,* there comes a state of silence that represents Absolute or transcendent Reality, Brahman.

avidya: Ignorance, lack of knowledge, mistaking the unreal for the real. The words avidya and maya in Vedanta philosophy refer to the force through which the universe evolves. At the individual level, it is called avidya; at the cosmic level, it is called maya. It is through this force that the pure, infinite, and immortal soul considers itself to be limited.

Bhagavad Gita: A celebrated text of Yoga which is part of a great epic called the *Mahabharata,* also called the "Song of God." The wisdom presented in the eighteen chapters of this text is in the form of a dialogue between Krishna (the teacher) and Arjuna (the student).

bhakti: Love and devotion; love for God. Bhakti is of two kinds: lower bhakti and higher bhakti. The lower bhakti consists of chanting the name of the lord, doing japa, reciting holy scriptures, serving God through one's thought, speech, and action; the higher bhakti is a state of ecstasy in which the yogi remains intoxicated in the love of the divine. Bhakti yoga is considered to be one of the major paths of yoga, since it places its main emphasis on love for God. All other disciplines are secondary to love and devotion to God,

bhava: Emotion, mood, devotional state of mind, feeling. This refers to the aspirant's emotional life, which in the practice of jnana or raja yoga, is controlled in order to transcend the spheres of mind and intellect. In bhakti yoga, however, bhava is neither controlled nor suppressed, but is transformed into devotion and channeled to the Lord.

Brahma: The Creator. According to Indian philosophy, the first evolute of unmanifest Brahman, the Absolute Reality, is Brahma, who through his sankalpa shakti brings forward all of creation. He is also the first teacher—the one who imparted the first spiritual wisdom to the sages.

brahmacharya: "Walking in Brahman," maintaining awareness of Brahman; controlling the senses, and celibacy. This also refers to the first stage of life, usually the first twenty-five years, in which a human being devotes his time and energy to studying and unveiling the mysteries of life here and hereafter.

brahmaloka: The realm of Brahman.

Brahman: The Absolute Reality, pure consciousness or the Truth that lies beyond names and forms. The Brahman of the Upanishads transcends the concept of God as found in most religions, being a pure witness and the only Reality. The universe emerges from Brahman and ultimately merges into Brahman. Throughout, Brahman is uninvolved and eternal—the underlying unitary Truth behind all diversities. The word Ishvara, or God, is the manifest state of Brahman. However, metaphysically, Brahman transcends the whole manifest world, including God.

brahmana: Brahmana should not be confused with the word Brahman, from which it is derived. Brahmana has two meanings: 1) it refers to a class of people who are inclined to spiritual study and practice, who devote their lives to attain brahman realization; 2) a group of Sanskrit texts devoted to the interpretation of Vedic hymns. In contrast to Upanishadic literature, brahmana texts provide a ritualistic interpretation and application of Vedic mantras.

brahmapuri: The seat, sphere, or abode of Brahman. In yoga shastra, sahasrara chakra is called brahmapuri.

brahma vidya: Knowledge or science of brahman; spiritual wisdom that leads an aspirant to the realization of Brahman consciousness. It is the knowledge of total existence, the highest Truth; according to the Upanishads, this science subsumes the knowledge of everything else. This is why after knowing this, "the unheard becomes heard, and the unknown becomes known."

Brahmin: During the Vedic period, this word meant "knower of Brahman" or "one who had devoted his entire life to the study of the Vedas and the realization of Brahman." In later periods, it referred to the priestly class in Indian society.

buddhi: Intellect; the faculty of discrimination. One of the aspects of the antahakarana, the inner faculty through which a human being makes decisions.

chakra: "Wheel," or center of consciousness. According to the Upanishads, there are seven centers of consciousness located along the spinal column: muladhara, svadhisthana, manipura, anahata, vishuddha, ajna, and sahasrara.

chaturmasa: The four months of the rainy season which, according to the Indian calendar, are the equivalent of our period of July through October. For these four months, the wandering sadhus stay in one place to perform their practices and impart knowledge to students who come to stay with them.

chhanda: Meter; those texts which describe the rules and regulations in regard to the meters in which Vedic mantras are composed.

chitta: Mind. The word chitta is a general term used for mind, which includes manas (lower mind), ahamkara (ego), and buddhi (intellect). Sometimes it is used in the sense of the unconscious mind, the storehouse of all the subtle impressions of one's thoughts, speech, and actions.

darshana: A vision, revelation, or a philosophy; to have a glance at a respected person, such as a sage.

deva: Celestial being, a bright being. According to the Upanishads, the powers of the senses are devas since they illuminate the objects of the world and bring them into the realm of experience and awareness. Indra, the god of the devas, is the mind, which presides over the other devas (the senses).

devayana: The path of light; vehicle of light; the path leading to the realm of bright beings. In the Upanishads, it is also called the solar path.

dharma: Duty; virtuous deeds, righteous acts, rules and laws that help one sustain personal as well as interpersonal well-being.

dhyana: Meditation; one-pointed state of mind that is not disturbed by any thought constructs.

dvapara yuga: The third of the four cycles of creation, in which the rituals first started and were considered the means to liberation.

ekarshi: One sage, the only seer, the fire of knowledge.

Gayatri mantra: The famous mantra that first appears in the *Yajur Veda:* it is considered to be the mother of all of the Vedas.

grahasthya: Householder's life; second stage of life.

guhachara: That which dwells in the cave of the heart; the inner light of at man.

guna: Intrinsic characteristic of prakriti, primordial nature; there are three gunas: sattva, rajas, and tamas.

guru (guru deva): Spiritual teacher. *Gu* means ignorance, *ru* means one who dispels. Thus, a guru is a learned master who dispels the darkness of a student's ignorance.

Hiranyagarbha: The shining being in whom the whole universe lives in its dormant state. Hiranyagarbha is also known as Brahma, the creator.

hota: Of the three priests to perform Vedic ceremonies, the one who offers the oblations into the fire, in the same manner that jiva, the individual self, offers all samskaras and vasanas into the fire of knowledge.

hridayagranthi: Hridaya is the heart, granthi is a knot; the knot at the heart; the knot of ignorance. Without destroying this knot, the knowledge of atman cannot be attained.

ishta purta: Ishta denotes the deeds that the householder performs in the world, including the fire ceremony and studying the Vedas. Purta means doing charitable works selflessly for the good of others, and serving others who need your help.

Ishvara: God; inner controller; the Lord. In Vedanta philosophy, Brahman accompanied by maya is called Ishvara. Therefore, Ishvara is called saguna Brahman.

ishvara pranidhana: Surrender to God. One of the components of the path of kriya yoga as outlined by Patanjali in the *Yoga Sutras.* However, according to bhakti yoga, surrender to God alone can lead one to the highest state of realization.

japa: Repetition of one's mantra; constant japa is a great technique of making the mind one-pointed. Japa as a practice is complete in itself provided it is done with knowledge and with full devotion.

jiva or jivatman: The individual soul is called jivatman as long as it uses the vehicle of the mind which, in association with ignorance (avidya), conceives itself to be limited.

jnana kanda: The portion of the Vedas concerning knowledge, as opposed to actions or ritual performances. Vedic literature is divided into two parts, karma kanda and jnana kanda. Brahmana literature belongs to the karma kanda, whereas the Upanishads belong to jnana kanda.

jnana yoga: The path of pure intellect; it is possible only when an aspirant purifies the higher buddhi.

kali yuga: The last of the four yugas (ages) in the cycle of creation, characterized by a decline of virtues and righteousness; faith and devotion are the means to liberation in the kali yuga.

kalpa: A measurement of Vedic time; a cycle divided into four yugas (ages). The characteristics of each kalpa are determined by the samskaras accumulated by human beings in the previous cycle.

karma: Action. Karma includes the law of actions and reactions, the driving forces of one's present and future. According to yoga traditions, karma that is performed with a selfish motive brings about bondage, while performing the same karma selflessly for the sake of duty alone brings freedom.

karma kanda: The portion of the Vedas concerning ritual performance, as opposed to the knowledge of Brahman.

karma mukti: A systematic and gradual path, step-by-step, to obtain liberation.

karma yoga: Path of selflessness. The "discipline of action" in which selfless action without desire for personal gain is cultivated. In this way one gradually cuts back on the number of new impressions (the seeds of future action and of rebirth). One's actions are gradually purified as meditation is slowly brought into active life.

karma yogi: One who has learned to do his or her duties as selfless actions and with attention constantly fixed on the center of consciousness within.

Kaula: A school of Tantra that emphasizes external rituals or uses eternal objects as means for spiritual achievement.

kosha(s): Sheath. The five levels of human existence. The five koshas or sheaths cover the effulgent Brahman or atman. They are the annamaya kosha (physical body), pranamaya kosha (energy sheath), manomaya kosha (mental or emotional sheath), jnanamaya kosha (intellectual sheath), and the anandamaya kosha (blissful sheath).

kriya: Action, activity, as kriya yoga—a path of action. In hatha and kundalini yoga, kriya refers to certain prana-yama and cleansing techniques; in Patanjali's system of yoga, it refers to the practice of austerity, self-study, and surrender to God.

kunda: The cavity at the base of the spinal column, in which the primal fire, kundalini, resides.

kundalini: The inner fire, the dormant fire, coiled energy. Kundalini in its dormant state resides at the base of the spine in an area called the kunda. By following a systematic discipline of pranayama, meditation, and mantra japa, one prepares oneself for kundalini awakening. At the completion of preparation, with the help of a competent master, this force is awakened and led to the sahasrara chakra where jivatman, the individual self, unites with Brahman.

lingam: Sign, symbol. Lingam also refers to the oval-shaped light that resides in the cave of the heart. In an external sense, it also refers to the shiva lingam. Symbolically, the shape of the individual soul is said to be like a lingam. Since Brahman is Absolute, without name or form, it is called *alingam.*

Mahabharata: Famous epic written in Sanskrit, consisting of 100,000 verses.

mahavakya: Great sayings from the Upanishads that deepen the inner awareness of the aspirant.

manas: Mind. One of the inner instruments that receive information from the external world with the help of the senses and present it to the higher faculty of intellect. This particular faculty is characterized by doubt.

manas puja: Mental worship. Students of the Mishra school of Tantra perform their rituals not at an external altar but rather at the heart center. Their entire worship is internal and thus is called mental worship.

manipura chakra: The chakra that is "filled with jewels"; naval center; the center of the fire element; the solar plexus.

manomaya kosha: The mental or emotional sheath. One of the five sheaths or koshas that cover the effulgent Brahman or atman.

mantra: There are two meanings for mantra: 1) Divine seed syllables which, through constant repetition and remembrance, lead students toward higher spiritual achievement.

A set of syllables, sounds, or words received from the teacher during initiation for meditation and spiritual advancement, and 2) the earliest part of Vedic literature, called mantra, or hymns, which is collected into four books, the *Rig*, *Yajur*, *Sama*, and *Atharva Vedas*.

mantra drastha: Seer of a mantra.

maya: The power of Brahman through which its infinity is veiled and the finite world is projected. On the cosmic level it is maya, on the individual level is it avidya.

Mishra: "Mixture or combination"; period of transition. There are three major schools of Tantra: Kaula, Mishra, and Samaya. Kaula employs external objects as means in its spiritual practice, and involves itself in external rituals. Samaya is a purely yogic path and does not rely on external means at all. The path of Mishra comes in between. A yogi belonging to the Mishra path internalizes all external rituals and meditates at the heart center.

moksha: Liberation; freedom from bondage. According to the Upanishads, the final stage of liberation can be attained only through knowledge of the Absolute, para vidya.

muladhara chakra: The root chakra at the base of the spine; the center for the earth element; the center that is the base of worship for the Kaula school of Tantra.

mundaka: "Shaven head"; denotes a monk.

Mundaka Upanishad: An Upanishad belonging to the *Atharva Veda* that is traditionally studied by monks.

nadi: Energy channel; one of the subtle channels of the body.

nirguna: Without attributes; pure transcendent Brahman, as opposed to saguna Brahman, Brahman with attributes.

panchopachara puja: Worship done with five articles: water, flowers, incense, the flame of a candle or ghee lamp, and an offering. In mental worship, the above-mentioned five articles are replaced by the five gross elements of earth, water, fire, air, and space, along with their corresponding subtle energies.

paramananda: Highest joy, as opposed to sensory pleasure.

paramatman: The highest Self, the Absolute Self; Brahman, the soul at the cosmic level, in contrast to jivatman, the soul at the individual level.

para vidya: Knowledge of the Absolute Truth, also known as brahma vidya, knowledge of Brahman. Knowledge of beyond, of the other shore, that helps the aspirant to realize the Absolute Truth and gain liberation.

parvati: Eternal consort of shiva; another name of shakti.

pramada: Inertia, laziness or sloth, and carelessness, which are the prime enemies of a sadhaka.

prana: The life force. In the yogic tradition, the life force prana is said to be tenfold, depending on its nature and function. Of the ten, prana and apana are the most important. Prana is ordinarily identified with inhalation and apana with exhalation. According to the *Bhagavad Gita*, a yogi should balance and control the movement of prana and apana in order to have control over the modifications of the mind and thus attain samadhi.

pranamaya kosha: Energy sheath. One of the five sheaths, or koshas, that cover the effulgent Brahman or atman.

pranayama: Expansion of, or voluntary control over the pranic force. Breath control; breathing exercise; the fourth rung of raja yoga. The science of gradually lengthening and controlling the physical breath in order to gain control over the movements of prana through the subtle body in higher stages of the practice. It is the fourth of the eight steps of yoga described by Patanjali.

prarabdha karma: One of three kinds of karma: prarabdha refers to the results being obtained from karmas that one has already performed; the karmas that germinate and bear fruit in this lifetime. Total freedom is not possible until all prarabdha karma is exhausted.

Prayoga Shastras: Section of Tantric literature that describes the particular application of mantras and yantras.

purusha: Pure Consciousness. "One who sleeps in the city of life." "That which fills all, that which dwells in the body (puranatvat)." The cosmic Self.

rajas: One of the three gunas that compose the universe and all in it; the rajasic aspect refers to the human aspect in man, in contrast to the animal and divine aspects in him. The rajasic guna is characterized by vibration, activity, and motion.

raja yoga: Royal path; the eightfold path of yoga as described by Patanjali in the *Yoga Sutras*.

Rig Veda: The earliest section of the Vedas, also known as *Rigveda Samhita*. The other three, the *Yajur, Sama,* and *Atharva Vedas,* derive more than half of their contents from the *Rig Veda*. This is the section that concerns itself with the mantras, along with the rules for their pronunciation and recitation.

rishi: Seer of a mantra.

sadhana: Practice, spiritual endeavor. Literally, "accomplishing," or "fulfilling." Sadhana is the word for a student's sincere efforts along a particular path of practice toward self-realization.

sadhya: A species of being that exists between humans and Gods.

saguna (Brahman): Brahman with attributes; Brahman combined with maya, also known as Ishvara, or God. This is a lower form of Brahman, in contrast to the highest which is nirguna Brahman, Brahman without attributes, or pure, transcendental reality.

sahasrara chakra: The crown chakra; the thousand-petalled lotus, located at the crown of the head.

sakama puja: Worship performed with a desire to attain some particular fruit, done for worldly motives; this puja yields success in the world, but not on the path of spirituality.

sakshatkara: The state of "seeing Truth face-to-face."

samadhi: Spiritual absorption; the eighth rung of raja yoga. The state in which the yogi is aware of the process of meditation, the object of meditation, and the meditator, is samadhi with seed. When the yogi merges into unitary consciousness, it is samadhi without seed.

Sama Veda: The second book of the Vedas. Most of the mantras of the *Sama Veda* are taken from the *Rig Veda*. The difference between them lies in the method of recitation. The *Sama Veda* is the origin of Indian classical music.

Samaya: This is considered to be the highest of the three schools of Tantra; the aspirants in this school perform internal worship using pranayama, meditation, and contemplation, rather than external rituals.

samsara: "That which continues without beginning or end"; the cycle of ignorance, desire, action, and longing to reap the fruits of the actions.

samskara: Subtle impressions of one's own past karmas, or actions. The innermost wall of the city of life is constructed by the samskaras that hold the aspirant's attachments and pleasure-seeking desires.

sanatana dharma: Eternal law as described in the Vedas and Upanishads.

sanchita karma: Collected or stored. This refers to the impressions of karma, stored in the form of vasanas, that have not yet started to produce fruit. When these karmas ripen to the stage of producing fruit, they are called prarabdha karma.

sannyasa: Renunciation. The fourth and final of the four stages of life.

satsanga: The company of saints and sages, which strengthens the aspirant's awareness of Brahman.

sattva: A guna (attribute of prakrti); one of the three gunas that compose the universe and all in it; the sattvic aspect refers to the divine aspect in man, in contrast to the animal and human aspects in him. Sattva guna is characterized by purity, luminosity, lightness, harmony, and the production of pleasure. It is the purest aspect of the three gunas.

satya yuga: The first of the four yugas (ages) in a cycle of creation. In the satya yuga, knowledge was the means to liberation.

Shabda Brahman: Brahman that manifests in the form of sound, shabda.

shakti: Divine force, power of Brahman, creative force of the Absolute Truth.

shantih: Peace.

shiva: Supreme Consciousness without any attributes.

shodashopachara puja: A worship that uses sixteen articles or ingredients. In internal worship, these sixteen articles are the five elements, the ten senses, and the mind.

shraddha: Faith; devotion combined with reverence. Faith is a divine quality and an essential aspect of one's spiritual practice. Such faith does not rely on the knowledge of the scriptures; rather it comes through spontaneous experience from within. Faith that samadhi is the only worthy goal and that one has chosen the way of self-realization.

shruti: Revealed knowledge, the Vedas.

siddhi: Accomplishment, perfection, achievement. In practicing yoga, as one progresses toward the center of consciousness, several supernatural capacities unfold, which can be very attractive and distracting. The goal of yoga is to not become caught by the siddhis, but to go beyond.

soma: An aspect of life-sustaining energy; that which fuels the fire of life. In the Upanishads, soma is said to drip from sahasrara chakra; it is imbibed by the coiled energy—kundalini shakti—at muladhara chakra, intoxicating her.

surya: The sun; solar energy.

sushumna: The central energy channel or nadi that runs along the spinal column from the base to the *brahmarandra,* at the crown of the head.

svadhisthana chakra: "Her own abode," the pelvic center.

svadhyaya: Self study, study of the Self, study by oneself, constant japa of the mantra received from a teacher, contemplating the meaning of the mahavakyas, the great sentences of the Upanishads.

tamas: One of the attributes of primordial nature, prakriti. Energy that tends to move downward. Its qualities are stability, stagnation, dullness, inertia, darkness, stasis, stupor.

Tantra: A particular school of yoga that is practiced in three successive stages: Kaula, Mishra, and Samaya. In Kaula, external objects and tools are used for spiritual enhancement; Mishra is a school of transition wherein an aspirant tries to internalize the external means; Samaya is purely an internal, yogic path in which the yogi meditates on sahasrara, the crown chakra.

Tantra Shastra: Tantric literature.

tapas: Loosely translated as austerities or penance, the word tapas literally means to shine, to glow, and heat. In a spiritual tradition, this word refers to the discipline that helps one to attain control over one's senses and mind, become vibrant, and overcome one's weaknesses. It is certainly different from penance or even austerity which, in religious contexts, usually implies self-mortification. The basic purpose of tapas is to transcend the pairs of opposites such as heat/cold and pleasure/pain, and at a physical level, unfold the hidden potentials of body, mind, and senses in order to become more creative in life.

tattva: Element. There are five elements: earth, water, fire, air, and space.

treta yuga: The second of the four yugas (ages) in a cycle of creation, characterized by the performance of tapas as a means to liberation.

turiya: The fourth, highest, transcendent state of consciousness. This refers to the experience of samadhi.

tyaga: Renouncing, giving up, non-attachment.

udgata: One of three priests in the Vedic ceremonies; the one whose function was to recite the mantras.

Upanishad: The last phase of the development of Vedic literature. The section of Vedic literature that emphasizes the path of knowledge.

vairagya: Dispassion; control over desires for worldly and other-worldly pleasures; state of being devoid of or free from attraction to objects reflecting into and coloring the mind; renunciation; disinterest in the world. Vairagya (dispassion) and abhyasa (practice) are the sine qua non of achievement on the yogic path.

vaisvadeva: All the Gods, shining beings of the universe, a group of Gods.

vanaprastha: Forest dwellers. The stage in life between grahasthya (householder) and sannyasa (renunciation). In this stage, an aspirant prepares himself for final renunciation.

vayu: Air; vital energy; breath. Vayu also refers to practices related to pranayama.

Veda: Knowledge; revealed scriptures; mantras that the seers received in their deep meditation; the sourcebook of knowledge. Knowledge in the Vedas is considered to be revealed wisdom, experienced by the great sages in deep meditation. For many centuries the sages imparted the knowledge of the Vedas orally to their close disciples. Finally the great sage Vyasa committed the Vedas to writing, organizing them into four classes on the basis of topic and practical application. These four sections are now known as the *Rig, Sama, Yajur,* and *Atharva Vedas.* The Upanishads are the last portions of these four books of the Vedas.

Vedanta: The system of Indian philosophy that expounds the theory of non-dualism.

Vedanta Sutras: First systematic written record of the Vedas as a philosophy, compiled by Vyasa.

vichara: Contemplation, right thinking, discrimination.

vidya: Knowledge. There are two kinds of vidya: para vidya, higher knowledge of Brahman, and apara vidya, the lower knowledge of the manifest aspect of reality.

vijnanamaya kosha: Sheath of intellect; the intellectual aspect of one's personality. One of the five sheaths or koshas that cover the effulgent Brahman or atman.

virat purusha: The great cosmic being.

vishayananda: Sensory pleasure, as opposed to the para-mananda or joy derived from samadhi.

vishuddha chakra: Throat center; center of the space element.

Vyasa: The famous sage and philosopher who is considered to be the author of all of the Puranas, the *Brahma Sutras*, and who also first compiled and organized Vedantic mantras. According to some scholars, Vyasa is the name of a tradition or institution devoted to philosophical and spiritual studies.

yajna: Ritual ceremony.

Yajur Veda: The section of the Vedas that is devoted mainly to ritual ceremonies and external worship.

yoga shastra: Yogic literature.

yuga: A measurement of time consisting of several thousand years.

Index

vairagya, 110, 156

vaisvadeva, 53, 156

vanaprasthya, 6, 7, 156

vayu, 113, 130, 156

Vedanta, 8, 9, 20, 128, 156

Vedanta Sutra, 20, 156–157

Vedas, 4–6, 8, 9, 12, 19, 20, 33, 34, 43, 44, 49, 53, 55, 63, 66, 77, 80–81, 130, 133, 134, 156

Vedas, date of, 9

Vedas, origin, 21

vegetarianism, 83–84

vichara, 93, 157

vidya, 12, 13, 19, 33, 48–49, 68–69, 157

vijnanamaya kosha, 102, 157

virat purusha, 79–81, 157

Virochana, 14

vishayananda, 62, 157

Vishnu, 40

vishuddha chakra, 51, 157

Vyasa, 5, 20, 157

water, 3, 38, 74, 76, 99, 101, 102, 110, 115, 120, 130–132, 134

worship, 6, 44, 51–55, 57–59, 61, 64, 90, 123, 134
 internal—Mishra, 52
 internal—Samaya, 52–53

yajna, 44, 58, 157

Yajur Veda, 5, 9, 34, 43, 80–81, 157

Yama, 13

yoga shastra, 157

yuga, 157

About Swami Rama

ONE OF THE greatest adepts, teachers, writers, and humanitarians of the 20th century, Swami Rama is the founder of the Himalayan Institute. Born in the Himalayas, he was raised from early childhood by the great Himalayan sage, Bengali Baba. Under the guidance of his master he traveled from monastery to monastery and studied with a variety of Himalayan saints and sages, including his grandmaster, who was living in a remote region of Tibet. In addition to this intense spiritual training, Swami Rama received higher education in both India and Europe. From 1949 to 1952, he held the prestigious position of Shankaracharya of Karvirpitham in South India. Thereafter, he returned to his master to receive further training at his cave monastery, and finally, in 1969, came to the United States, where he founded the Himalayan Institute. His best-known work, *Living with the Himalayan Masters*, reveals the many facets of this singular adept and demonstrates his embodiment of the living Himalayan Tradition.

HIMALAYAN INSTITUTE®

The main building of the Himalayan Institute headquarters near Honesdale, Pennsylvania

The Himalayan Institute

A leader in the field of yoga, meditation, spirituality, and holistic health, the Himalayan Institute is a nonprofit international organization dedicated to serving humanity through educational, spiritual, and humanitarian programs. The mission of the Himalayan Institute is to inspire, educate, and empower all those who seek to experience their full potential.

Founded in 1971 by Swami Rama of the Himalayas, the Himalayan Institute and its varied activities and programs exemplify the spiritual heritage of mankind that unites East and West, spirituality and science, ancient wisdom and modern technology.

Our international headquarters is located on a beautiful 400-acre campus in the rolling hills of the Pocono Mountains of northeastern Pennsylvania. Our spiritually vibrant community and peaceful setting provide the perfect atmosphere for seminars and retreats, residential programs, and holistic health services. Students from all over the world join us to attend diverse programs on subjects such as hatha yoga, meditation, stress reduction, ayurveda, and yoga and tantra philosophy.

In addition, the Himalayan Institute draws on roots in the yoga tradition to serve our members and community through the following programs, services, and products:

Mission Programs

The essence of the Himalayan Institute's teaching mission flows from the timeless message of the Himalayan Masters, and is echoed in our on-site mission programming. Their message is to first become aware of the reality within ourselves, and then to build a bridge between our inner and outer worlds.

Our mission programs express a rich body of experiential wisdom and are offered year-round. They include seminars, retreats, and professional certifications that bring you the best of an authentic yoga tradition, addressed to a modern audience. Join us on campus for our Mission Programs to find wisdom from the heart of the yoga tradition, guidance for authentic practice, and food for your soul.

Wisdom Library and Mission Membership

The Himalayan Institute online Wisdom Library curates the essential teachings of the living Himalayan Tradition. This offering is a unique counterpart to our in-person Mission Programs, empowering students by providing online learning resources to enrich their study and practice outside the classroom.

Our Wisdom Library features multimedia blog content, livestreams, podcasts, downloadable practice resources, digital courses, and an interactive Seeker's Forum. These teachings capture our Mission Faculty's decades of study, practice, and teaching experience, featuring new content as well as the timeless teachings of Swami Rama and Pandit Rajmani Tigunait.

We invite seekers and students of the Himalayan Tradition to become a Himalayan Institute Mission Member, which grants unlimited access to the Wisdom Library. Mission Membership offers a way for you to support our shared commitment to service, while deepening your study and practice in the living Himalayan Tradition.

Spiritual Excursions

Since 1972, the Himalayan Institute has been organizing pilgrimages for spiritual seekers from around the world. Our spiritual excursions follow the traditional pilgrimage routes where adepts of the Himalayas lived and practiced. For thousands of years, pilgrimage has been an essential part of yoga sadhana, offering spiritual seekers the opportunity to experience the transformative power of living shrines of the Himalayan Tradition.

Global Humanitarian Projects

The Himalayan Institute's humanitarian mission is yoga in action—offering spiritually grounded healing and transformation to the world. Our humanitarian projects serve impoverished communities in India, Mexico, and Cameroon through rural empowerment and environmental regeneration. By putting yoga philosophy into practice, our programs are empowering communities globally with the knowledge and tools needed for a lasting social transformation at the grassroots level.

Publications

The Himalayan Institute publishes over 60 titles on yoga, philosophy, spirituality, science, ayurveda, and holistic health. These include the best-selling books *Living with the Himalayan Masters* and *The Science of Breath*, by Swami Rama; *The Power of Mantra and the Mystery of Initiation, From Death to Birth, Tantra Unveiled,* and two commentaries on the *Yoga Sutra—The Secret of the Yoga Sutra: Samadhi Pada* and *The Practice of the Yoga Sutra: Sadhana Pada*— by Pandit Rajmani Tigunait, PhD; and the award-winning *Yoga: Mastering the Basics* by Sandra Anderson and Rolf Sovik, PsyD. These books are for everyone: the interested reader, the spiritual novice, and the experienced practitioner.

PureRejuv Wellness Center

For over 40 years, the PureRejuv Wellness Center has fulfilled part of the Institute's mission to promote healthy and sustainable lifestyles. PureRejuv combines Eastern philosophy and Western medicine in an integrated approach to holistic health—nurturing balance and healing at home and at work. We offer the opportunity to find healing and renewal through on-site wellness retreats and individual wellness services, including therapeutic massage and bodywork, yoga therapy, ayurveda, biofeedback, natural medicine, and one-on-one consultations with our integrative medical staff.

Total Health Products

The Himalayan Institute, the developer of the original Neti Pot, manufactures a health line specializing in traditional and modern ayurvedic supplements and body care. We are dedicated to holistic and natural living by providing products using non-GMO components, petroleum-free biodegrading plastics, and eco-friendly packaging that has the least impact on the environment. Part of every purchase supports our Global Humanitarian projects, further developing and reinforcing our core mission of spirituality in action.

For further information about our programs, humanitarian projects, and products:

call: 800.822.4547
e-mail: info@HimalayanInstitute.org
write: The Himalayan Institute
         952 Bethany Turnpike
         Honesdale, PA 18431
or visit: HimalayanInstitute.org

We are grateful to our members for their passion and commitment to share our mission with the world. Become a Mission Member and inherit the wisdom of a living tradition.

HIMALAYAN INSTITUTE®

inherit the wisdom of a living tradition today!

As a Mission Member, you will gain exclusive access to our online Wisdom Library. The Wisdom Library includes monthly livestream workshops, digital practicums and eCourses, monthly podcasts with Himalayan Institute Mission Faculty, and multimedia practice resources.

Mission Membership Benefits

Wisdom Library

Netra Tantra: Harnessing the Healing Force (Part 1)
Pandit Rajmani Tigunait, PhD | September 28, 2017
Read more

- **Never-before-seen content from Swami Rama & Pandit Tigunait**
- **New content announcements & weekly blog roundup**
- **Unlimited access to online yoga classes and meditation classes**
- **Members only digital workshops and monthly livestreams**
- **Downloadable practice resources and Prayers of the Tradition**

Get FREE access to the Wisdom Library for 30 days!

Mission Membership is an invitation to put your spiritual values into action by supporting our shared commitment to service while deepening your study and practice in the living Himalayan Tradition.

BECOME A MISSION MEMBER AT:
himalayaninstitute.org/mission-membership/

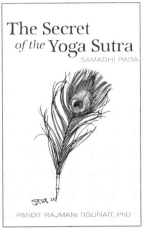

The Secret of the Yoga Sutra
Samadhi Pada
Pandit Rajmani Tigunait, PhD

The Yoga Sutra is the living source wisdom of the yoga tradition, and is as relevant today as it was 2,200 years ago when it was codified by the sage Patanjali. Using this ancient yogic text as a guide, we can unlock the hidden power of yoga, and experience the promise of yoga in our lives. By applying its living wisdom in our practice, we can achieve the purpose of life: lasting fulfillment and ultimate freedom.

Paperback, 6" x 9", 331 pages
$24.95, ISBN 978-0-89389-277-7

The Practice of the Yoga Sutra
Sadhana Pada
Pandit Rajmani Tigunait, PhD

In Pandit Tigunait's practitioner-oriented commentary series, we see this ancient text through the filter of scholarly understanding and experiential knowledge gained through decades of advanced yogic practices. Through *The Secret of the Yoga Sutra* and *The Practice of the Yoga Sutra*, we receive the gift of living wisdom he received from the masters of the Himalayan Tradition, leading us to lasting happiness.

Paperback, 6" x 9", 389 Pages
$24.95, ISBN 978-0-89389-279-1

Touched by Fire
Pandit Rajmani Tigunait, PhD

This vivid autobiography of a remarkable spiritual leader—Pandit Rajmani Tigunait, PhD—reveals his experiences and encounters with numerous teachers, sages, and his master, the late Swami Rama of the Himalayas. His well-told journey is filled with years of disciplined study and the struggle to master the lessons and skills passed to him. *Touched by Fire* brings Western culture a glimpse of Eastern philosophies in a clear, understandable fashion, and provides numerous photographs showing a part of the world many will never see for themselves.

Paperback with flaps, 6" x 9", 296 pages
$16.95, ISBN 978-0-89389-239-5

At the Eleventh Hour
Pandit Rajmani Tigunait, PhD

This book is more than the biography of a great sage—it is a revelation of the many astonishing accomplishments Swami Rama achieved in his life. These pages serve as a guide to the more esoteric and advanced practices of yoga and tantra not commonly taught or understood in the West. And they bring you to holy places in India, revealing why these sacred sites are important and how to go about visiting them. The wisdom in these stories penetrates beyond the power of words.

Paperback with flaps, 6" x 9", 448 pages
$18.95, ISBN 978-0-89389-211-1

Perennial Psychology of the Bhagavad Gita
Swami Rama

With the guidance and commentary of Himalayan Master Swami Rama, you can explore the wisdom of the Bhagavad Gita, which allows one to be vibrant and creative in the external world while maintaining a state of inner tranquility. This commentary on the Bhagavad Gita is a unique opportunity to see the Gita through the perspective of a master yogi, and is an excellent version for practitioners of yoga meditation. Spiritual seekers, psychotherapists, and students of Eastern studies will all find a storehouse of wisdom in this volume.

Paperback, 6" x 9", 479 pages
$19.95, ISBN 978-0-89389-090-2

Fearless Living: Yoga and Faith
Swami Rama

Learn to live without fear—to trust a higher power, a divine purpose. In this collection of anecdotes from the astonishing life of Swami Rama, you will understand that there is a way to move beyond mere faith and into the realm of personal revelation. Through his astonishing life experiences we learn about ego and humility, see how to overcome fears that inhibit us, discover sacred places and rituals, and learn the importance of a one-pointed, positive mind. Swami Rama teaches us to see with the eyes of faith and move beyond our self-imposed limitations.

Paperback with flaps, 6" x 9", 160 pages
$12.95, ISBN 978-0-89389-251-7

Meditation and Its Practice
Swami Rama

In this practical guide to inner life, Swami Rama teaches us how to slip away from the mental turbulence of our ordinary thought processes into an infinite reservoir of consciousness. This clear, concise meditation manual provides systematic guidance in the techniques of meditation - a powerful tool for transforming our lives and increasing our experience of peace, joy, creativity, and inner tranquility.

Paperback, 6" x 9", 128 pages
$12.95, ISBN 978-0-89389-153-4

The Art of Joyful Living
Swami Rama

In *The Art of Joyful Living*, Swami Rama imparts a message of inspiration and optimism: that you are responsible for making your life happy and emanating that happiness to others. This book shows you how to maintain a joyful view of life even in difficult times.

It contains sections on transforming habit patterns, working with negative emotions, developing strength and willpower, developing intuition, spirituality in loving relationships, learning to be your own therapist, understanding the process of meditation, and more!

Paperback, 6" x 9", 198 pages
$15.95, ISBN 978-0-89389-236-4

Tantra Unveiled
Pandit Rajmani Tigunait, PhD

This powerful book describes authentic tantra, what distinguishes it from other spiritual paths, and how the tantric way combines hatha yoga, meditation, visualization, ayurveda, and other disciplines. Taking us back to ancient times, Pandit Tigunait shares his experiences with tantric masters and the techniques they taught him. *Tantra Unveiled* is most valuable for those who wish to live the essence of tantra—practicing spirituality while experiencing a rich outer life.

Paperback, 6" x 9", 152 pages
$14.95, ISBN 978-0-89389-158-9

Moving Inward
Rolf Sovik, PsyD

Rolf Sovik shows readers of all levels how to transition from asanas to meditation. Combining practical advice on breathing and relaxation with timeless asana postures, he systematically guides us through the process. This book provides a five-stage plan to basic meditation, step-by-step guidelines for perfect postures, and six methods for training the breath. Both the novice and the advanced student will benefit from Sovik's startling insights into the mystery of meditation.

Paperback, 6" x 9", 197 pages
$14.95, ISBN 978-0-89389-247-0